# For Those Who Wonder

## Observations on Faith, Belief, Doubt, Reason, and Knowledge

3rd Printing

by D. Jeff Burton
178 No. Alta Street
Salt Lake City, Utah 84103

Foreword by Lowell L. Bennion

IVE, Inc
Salt Lake City, Utah

Published by IVE, Inc., Salt Lake City, Utah



D. Jeff Burton
178 No. Alta Street
Salt Lake City, Utah  84103

ISBN:  (0-9623160-4-0)

Published in the United States.

10 9 8 7 6 5 4 3

Note:  All names and places referred to in short stories are fictional. Any similarity to real persons or places is unintentional andcoincidental.

# Acknowledgements

I want to thank Lowell Bennion, a trusted friend and counselor, and Lavina Fielding Anderson, who thoughtfully edited the text. Others helped: Scott Dunn, Richard Poll, Suzanne Dean, Phillip Barlow, and Ross Jones.

Since the first edition in 1986, many people have phoned, or have sent letters. I have learned much, and my life has been enriched.

Thank you.

## FOREWORD

### by Lowell L. Bennion

Life on the planet earth is wonderfully complex. From the dawn of consciousness, human beings have tried to understand it. But they have also gone further by trying to understand it in absolute terms. They have sought to know the truth.

Yet truth is not part of the reality we are trying to understand. Truth exists in the minds of persons--of Deity and human beings. The earth, for example, is what it is. To the degree that our ideas about the earth correspond to or agree with what the earth really is, to that extent we have the truth about the earth. Or to take another example, God is what he is. To the extent that our ideas about God correspond to what he really is, to that extent we have the truth about God. It is obvious that we do not have the whole truth about God.

Human beings have developed several different ways of knowing reality, of finding the truth: (1) by thinking, or rationalism; (2) by experience, or empiricism; (3) by revelation from Deity; and (4) by intuition. Sometimes revelation may come as a form of intuition.

These different ways of knowing have developed symbolic systems of thought and feeling--philosophy, science, religion, the arts, and so forth. It is natural for these different ways of knowing to come up with different views of the same reality and to be critical of one another's conclusions. For centuries there has been tension between faith (religion) and reason (philosophy and science).

These differing points of view have sometimes caused bright and thoughtful people to question their faith and to doubt something they have been taught in the church. The author of this work, D. Jeff Burton, has rich and extensive experience counseling people who are troubled because thinking has led them to question and even doubt some things they have learned in a religious setting.

When conflict develops between a man's (or woman's) faith and his thinking, one of three things can happen. He can quit thinking and hold fast to faith. Or, he can put trust in reason and reject faith. A third, and for me a better solution, is to recognize the important roles both thinking and faith play in life and to try to understand and respect the role of each one.

Burton has brought together a collection of his stories and essays dealing with problems of faith and knowledge. By using both fiction and reasoned discourse, he is recognizing and appealing to more than one of the ways by which we seek understanding. In an annotated bibliographic essay, he quotes thoughtful Mormon writers: Joseph Smith, Orson Pratt, James E. Talmage, Richard Poll, and Jan Stout. He also quotes from some well respected non-Mormon writers: William James, Bertrand Russell, Eric Hoffer, Paul Tillich, Francisco Jose Moreno, and James Fowler. All are deep thinkers. Their writings stimulate thought rather than draw definite conclusions. This collection of stories and essays does the same. It will appeal to those who think and question; it may even disturb the comfortable believer; but it will teach them new ways of thinking as they find limitations in the old ways.

The last chapter, Burton's "Helping Those with Religious Doubts and Questions," is replete with constructive suggestions on how to cope with doubt.

A poem by Margaret Rampton Munk to me expresses the author's purpose better than I.

**A Skeptic's Prayer**

Is it true
Thou lovest best
Thy meek, unasking children?

Thou has made us

So diverse, so various,
Yet in the image of a Sire
Who filled the universe
With His creative fire.

What father has supposed
His child would grow to manhood

Only hearing and affirming?
What man could honor such a son?
How could a mind that,
Like a Sponge,
Absorbs but never questions,
Doubts,
Or wonders why
Be offspring and apprentice
To a God?

It may be, Lord,
Thou canst never love me.
With the calm relief
a father feels
For his obedient child--
The one who's never any trouble.

But use me
As a bridge
To those more wayward still
Than I.
I cannot give them all the answers;
But they will not ask
The ones who think they can.

Let me speak
To Thy lost sheep
As one who,
Understanding how they went astray,
Still loves the Shepherd.

--Margaret Rampton Munk*

* *So Far* (n.p.: privately printed, 1986), p. 59. Used by permission.

## CONTENTS

# INTRODUCTION

The essays and short stories in this collection are intended for Mormons who wonder about their religious life, and for their friends and relatives who would like to understand what they are experiencing.

My private impression is that five to ten percent of active Mormons actually disbelieve important tenets of our religion, and that about 25-30 per cent have ever-present questions and doubts. Furthermore, many firm believers experience episodes of doubting and questioning--trials of their faith.

Questioning and wondering are normally healthy--they motivate us to action and study. Unfortunately, many of us suffer unnecessarily from feelings of guilt, inadequacy, depression, and estrangement. I hope this book will console, hearten, and ease the pain for those who wonder. I also hope it will make it easier for us to ask questions when necessary.

This book, a mixture of essays and fiction, is deliberately unconventional. It is designed to encourage browsing. Many readers prefer essays while others enjoy fiction. Some concepts are handled best through analysis and rational argument while a human predicament will cut to the heart of still other issues. I suggest that you read the articles and stories you enjoy, and leave the others. Because each essay and story stands by itself, you can begin anywhere. If you enjoy intellectual pursuits, you might want to begin at the end of the book with "A Bibliographic Essay (Chapter 15), and then read "Wonderful Wondering." (Chapter 3) "Helping those with Religious Questions and Doubts" may give you a place to begin if you're dealing with a friend or loved one experiencing a crisis of faith. If you like fiction, the story "A Twenty-first Century Call" explores what might trigger a crisis for many. If you like analysis of human behavior, try "The Phenomenon of the Closet Doubter." If you have recently been devastated by sudden doubts and questions, you might begin with "The Gift" and "The Evidence of Things Not Seen."

I consider my writing to be a dialogue. You have an open invitation to make it a real one by sharing with me your thoughts and experiences.

D. Jeff Burton
178 No. Alta Street
Salt Lake City, Utah 84103

## Chapter 1

## The Phenomenon of the Closet Doubter

*The following essay was presented at the 1982 Sunstone Theological Symposium. It appeared in* Sunstone, *September 1982.*

Mormons pride themselves on being a tight-knit group. But there are groups within the group--investigators, believers, non-believers, jack-Mormons, the faithful, temple recommend holders, cultural Mormons, "inside-outsiders," the active, and so forth. I would like to add another group to the list--"closet doubters." Other suitable names could include faithful doubters, faithful disbelievers, active disbelievers, or hopeful doubters.

During my mission to Japan in the early sixties, I chanced upon a superactive, but genuine non-believer--my first encounter with a faithful doubter. She was serving in the Young Women's Mutual leadership and was extremely active in the branch. I had been talking to her about bringing her non-member friends and, in the course of conversation, learned the secret of her disbelief.

I thought at the time that an active non-believer must be a rarity. But it was like learning a new word--what I had thought was a rare condition, I now recognized all around me. Since that day, I have had the opportunity to cautiously identify and speak confidentially with a number of people who have invisible memberships in the group I call closet doubters.

What is a closet doubter? A closet doubter, as I choose to define it, is an active Latter-day Saint who has secretly rejected (or disbelieves) one or more of the fundamental tenets upon which the Church is based, such as Joseph's first vision, his divine calling as a prophet of God, the Book of Mormon as an angel-delivered history of early Americans, or the divine origin of Joseph Smith's later revelations as published in the Doctrine and Covenants and Pearl of Great Price. But despite this secret disbelief, the closet doubter continues to be active in the Church. He or she attends meetings, teaches classes, holds a temple recommend, serves in presidencies, and may even be employed by the Church. Outwardly they are little different than other active believers. Closet doubters have not lost both belief and activity, nor do they announce their disbelief.

Most closet doubters I have met were in their late teens to mid-forties. Younger people apparently have neither the experience nor the education necessary to catalyze the complex reactions necessary to become closet doubters. Those I have known tended to be educated and well read. Most have studied the scriptures and appear well-versed in Church history. Some come from strong Church backgrounds. They are often the offspring of traditional Mormon parents, or they have been committed converts. Some have served missions and others have married in the temple. Most have had close and important ties to the Church such as church jobs or church callings.

What do they believe, how did they become doubters, and why do they stay active? Personal belief seems to be a continuum and is in a constant state of flux. The extremes are represented by "I know (something) is true" and "I know (something) is not true." The typical Church member professes a positive belief in the Joseph Smith story. Closet doubters, by my definition, must secretly admit to disbelief or negative belief. But--and this is a most interesting condition--most closet doubters seem to have had some belief before becoming doubters. Most, although doubting, express commitments to the goals, principles, and practices of today's Church. They often state their reasoning this way: The basic principles of the Church come from the Bible and thus are not the invention of Joseph Smith. Principles of love, caring, sharing, kindness, honesty, integrity, and sacrifice are universal, true, noble, believable, and worthy of support. Programs of education, health, and public service are worth supporting. The Church may not be true in the "one and only true church" sense, but there's nothing better. Few expect to find any "true church," and, in fact, are not looking. Settled closet doubters, although not untroubled, seem to be relatively happy, fulfilled people, with little hint of hate or vindictiveness.

This serenity is remarkable, given the anguish most experience during their "de-conversion." Before finally admitting to a lack of belief, many experience an agonizing transition period, usually measured in years and often filled with insecurity, alienation, anger, and confusion. This transition state is accompanied by feelings of guilt ("I mustn't feel this way," or "I shouldn't have felt critical of Brother X," or "I get upset reading Church History--why do I keep doing it?"), feelings of denial ("Of course I believe," or "Its just a test," or "I've got to stop thinking this way"), feelings of shame ("What kind of a sinner must I be?"), feelings of anger ("Why me?"), and feelings of loneliness ("I'm the only one with these thoughts and problems," or "There is no one who understands"). Given these emotional conflicts, it is not hard to understand why some seek professional counseling.

After finally facing up to the fact of their disbelief, most say they feel an odd sense of relief and a freedom not felt during the transition. They say things like, "The truth has made me free," and "Free agency finally means something." Some feel good in making a free choice to participate, without the guilt that hovered over them during the transition. Some express an understanding of their circumstances and are able to accept, even to cherish, this understanding. This is not to say that confirmed closet doubters are free from inner conflict. Far from it. The conflict just takes another form and is usually more tolerable.

No doubter's motives for continued activity are as pure and idealistic as I have just described. Most doubters are tied to the Church like birds are to mother earth. It might be possible to fly high, but gravity eventually has its way. These gravitational ties include being married to a believing spouse, the desire to give children strong and stable support, family traditions and history ("It would hurt my mother if I went inactive"), job security and pension programs (when employed by the Church or BYU), a social life revolving around friends who are believers ("How do you attend your friend's temple wedding if you're inactive?"), and of course fear ("The official Joseph Smith story might be true, after all").

Some justify their continued activity as contributing to improvements in Church practices they consider weak, wrong, or embarrassing. Those often mentioned include the black/priesthood issue (now resolved), the temple ceremony, women's rights, the stress on unquestioning obedience, and the lack of vertical dialogue from local members to general leaders. Many express feelings of hope--hope that perhaps in the great scheme of things God indeed recognizes and gives special status to the Church; hope that perhaps they can find peace; hope that they can do some good through the programs of the Church; and hope that perhaps they are wrong about their doubts.

Where are they? How many are there? And why do we hear so little about them? I believe they're everywhere in well-established Church locales, but they're probably more concentrated in the larger cities, on university campuses, and in the more affluent and educated wards. As for numbers, there is no way of knowing.

What predisposes one to become a faithful doubter? How does one lose long-term beliefs? These are difficult questions and I do not have the answers. But education seems to be a contributing factor. Others include intellectual liveliness, difficulties with authoritarian leadership, and "male-dominated" leadership. Knowledge of Church history seems to be common. Access to anti-Church literature is often present. It is difficult, however, to tell which comes first, the doubts, which lead to search for confirmation, or the detracting literature, which leads to a loss of belief. I have noticed that for many people, it is a stepped process: a little doubt supported by a little justification leading to more doubt, the search for more justification, and so forth.

What impact do they have on the Church? There is no way of knowing, except to observe that doubters are involved in events at the local level and, because of their education and skills, they often have positions of leadership and influence.

Here are the statements of several closet doubters. To protect their identities I have changed some details of age, location, and employment, and some are composites of several people.

Ann is a late-thirties housewife, mother of three, college graduate, and a relief society teacher:

> By the time I finally recognized my lack of belief, my children were in school. My children don't need any disruptions in their lives at this time. It's hard enough. My husband is a ward leader. What alternatives do I have? If I start talking honestly now, it could hurt his work. I'm not unhappy. I just find it easier to keep quiet about the whole thing. My husband is very good about it, although I don't think he really understands. He thinks I'm going through a stage, a trial of my faith. It's easier for me to let him think that. Anyway, maybe I am. I hope he's right.

Bill is a 40-year old high priest, married, has two children, and is a college graduate:

> The big thing left for me now is hope. I hope, I pray that things will turn out right. I hope the Church is true, but I really doubt it. It's worth staying with. Faith and hope. It's all I have, all I need, truly.

Ned is a mid-thirties salesman, divorced and re-married, and has had some college:

> My contact with the world started my journey into doubt. I went

> through terrible years of guilt and hate. I was impossible to live with. I lost my first wife over this, so I find it easier now to keep quiet. It's not my place to be going around destroying others' faith. The Lord showed me the light. Let him show others if that is what the Lord wants for them. Who's to say what the big picture is? I'm the last to say I have all the answers.

Len is a member of a bishopric. He is a husband and father of four children;he has an MBA and works as a business executive,:

> I have thought of quitting it all. But every time I do, all the positives seem to outweigh the negatives. I can influence things in my ward, but I have to be really careful not to do anything to embarrass the bishop. I try to stress the positive aspects of the gospel--sharing, love, giving. You know, those things that people really need. I always keep the Word of wisdom, pay my tithing, and, you know, that kind of stuff. But I do it because of my position and for my wife and kids. My kids don't know a thing, but my wife knows everything. In a way, she's coming to see things from my point of view...starting to support me in subtle ways.

Lila is 22-years old, single, a convert of six years now serving in a singles' ward activity program, and a student of biology:

> I joined because of my friends. The only friends I have now are in the Church. If I start causing trouble, I'll lose my friends. I know it sounds childish. But my parents were very upset when I joined. I don't have close ties back at home anymore. I hope to marry a Mormon. And nobody wants an inactive Mormon.

Stuart is a single, recently returned missionary, presently studying history at a Utah college. He is partly active with no Church calling:

> I never did gain that burning testimony everybody kept talking about. In fact, my belief in Joseph Smith disappeared during my mission. It's just too incredible! My mom and dad spent a lot of money . . . most of their savings to send me to England. If they knew . . . well, it would hurt them. I think I'll be pretty active. I'm not searching for a quick fix from anybody. The Church is my life and my guide. I'm just going to be cool and use what's good for me.

Susan is 28, a Ph.D. candidate, and serves in her ward primary. She recently married a non-Mormon man:

> Father in Heaven has answered my prayer--the Church teaches Christian principles but it isn't perfect. But before I received those answers it was rough. I didn't know who to turn to or who might help. I hope to get my husband to join. I feel a lot of peace with myself, knowing that I love the Church for its people and for what it can do for people, not for what is was, or purports to be.

Closet doubters keep their interpretations hidden. Sometimes, even spouses do not know the extent of their doubts. Why the need for secrecy? First, there is the fear of being ostracized, or worse, put in the "handle with care" category reserved for investigators. Mainstream believers often remain aloof and feel uncomfortable around those who ask too many questions or demonstrate a doubting nature. More seriously, believing members often interpret a rejection of their beliefs as a rejection of themselves. The second reason for secrecy is the fear that their chance for meaningful Church participation might be reduced. More than a few worry that an unsympathetic bishop might deny them a temple recommend, even though several I have talked to have confided in bishops who have been supportive and understanding. Third, the Church has said it can tolerate divergent beliefs as long as those beliefs are held personally and no attempt is made to sway others. This is interpreted to mean "Please keep you doubts to yourself." Finally, many express the thought that it is not their place to alter the beliefs of others. Coming out of the closet may be too great a shock for those whose testimonies rely on the strength of another's beliefs.

Doubters learn to speak truthfully but discreetly. When asked to bear testimony, they may say something like, "I know the Church teaches correct principles; I know that the Lord answers prayers; He loves every person; We must all work out our own salvation." Can they accept the president of the Church as a prophet, seer, and revelator? Some say, "Why not? Certainly no one else speaks for God," or "I can accept the possibility that he is a prophet." Others may say, "I accept, with what faith I have."

The need to maintain secrecy, to sometimes practice a subtle dishonesty, isolates the doubter and creates internal conflict. Such conflicts are the successors to those experienced during the often hellish time of transition.

Can closet doubters maintain this equilibrium in the Church? I believe so. Most I have met appeared relatively stable and happy, although some have since become inactive. Some have come out of the closet. Some have experienced a period of inactivity, then returned to activity again, still doubting but with renewed hope and faith. One person has developed a strong belief again.

As for the future, several scenarios have been suggested to me. The first, somewhat farfetched, proposes that in time some will reach positions of sufficient authority to modify claims made for Joseph Smith. Another scenario has their numbers and influence growing over the next few generations until the LDS Church somewhat resembles the Catholic Church with a large percentage who do not truly believe all of the official story but who stay and participate because of inertia, culture, tradition, and family. A third scenario pictures the Church somehow inviting and accepting disbelievers into open, full, and active fellowship. None of these imagined events seem very realistic or attractive.

*Addition to the third printing:* The Church has conducted systematic investigations of belief, faith, and activity among active members. The results have not been made available to the general public, as far as I know. It is my own private sense that the extent of skeptical thinking is expanding, particularly among the youth of the Church. The reality of increasing skepticism among members should not and cannot be overlooked forever. We will have to face up to it, and the sooner the better. As William James put it, "He who acknowledges the imperfections of his instrument, and makes allowance for it, is in a much better position for gaining (and sustaining) truth than if he claimed his instrument to be infallible" (*Varieties of Religious Experience,* 1902).

Even though the numbers of doubters may be increasing (and perhaps *because* of the increase), I believe it is actually easier for a faithful skeptic to be accepted among unruffled believers than in past years. I also think it is now easier to come out of the closet. And I believe it is useful to do so, and encourage secret doubters to prepare themselves and their families for that step.

I also see benefits in being faithful--particularly to oneself and to God, but also to the Church. The Church asks us to believe incredible things. But it also provides wonderful blessings. Those blessings are available to members who remain faithful to the teachings of Christ, and who continue participation in the Church. Additionally, inactive troubled people can have little effect on the things that trouble them. If you want to change things, you have to participate.

But, again, activity is a personal decision and everyone must eventually choose the path which makes most sense.

If you would like a dialogue with me, please write.

# Chapter 2

## Twenty-First Century Call

*I think we may safely trust a good deal more than we do.*
— Henry David Thoreau

*Note: There is a saying that rich men feel no temptation to steal bread. In a similar way, powerful men often feel no temptation to question the system which grants them power. This is the story of a man's struggle to maintain his faith at the time of personal stress. The story was originally published in* Exponent II.

The elevator slowed to a stop at the third floor of the old Church Administration Building. The elderly operator turned the key in the elevator control panel. "Nice to have known you folks," he said with a smile. Responding to his passengers' blank looks, he said more seriously, "Men are never the same after they receive a call from the Third Floor."

R. Grant Ellison and Sister Ellison stepped hesitantly into the spacious old lobby. The deep carpet, rich burgundy-and-white sculptured wool, was still beautiful after many years of use. Well-rubbed oak trim and hand-painted, off-white wall paper covered the walls, and heavy lace curtains from an earlier era framed large wooden windows overlooking South Temple Street.

Darkened oil paintings of early Church leaders hung heavily on the west wall, while glass cases displayed originals of the Book of Mormon and other early Church documents on the east. Light from the ancient cases cast a warm incandescent yellow glow on the wall behind. The lobby itself had been partially remodeled—ten years ago now—and was presently lit by a blue-white laser chandelier. The new clashed uncomfortably with the old in Ellison's thought: I'll take the traditional any time.

R. Grant Ellisòn stood quietly, his faithful wife and companion at his side. Tall, handsome, still muscular, graying at the temples, and dressed in a tailored, dark gray suit, he looked much like a bank president or Congressman. He shifted his weight to his right foot—his left ankle had been bothering him since his thirties, and hurt under a full load. Elevating the foot helped, but that was unthinkable here.

A large double door opened. A woman came through, nodded to the receptionist, then hurried out. Shortly, a gentle elderly man shuffled through the door. Ellison had never been in the man's presence before, but he immediately recognized President Wells, the seventy-six year old prophet, seer, and revelator for the Mormon Church, now 36 million members strong. Grant legs stiffened and his cheeks flushed. He took Sister Ellison's arm, knowing that she'd be needing support.

Sensing the tension, President Wells spoke in a soft, reassuring tone. "I'm sorry to keep you waiting. I've been looking forward to seeing you. Please, come in." President Wells grasped the arms of the Ellisons, separating them. With his thin hands at their waists, President Wells gently led them into his office toward three high-backed chairs at the side of his large, glass-topped desk. Directly in front of the desk was a dark leather chair obviously used for ordinations and blessings.

Ellison had not spoken a word. What can one say to a Prophet of God, he thought? What kind of small talk wouldn't sound…small?

President Wells asked them to turn their chairs so that they sat facing each other. Their knees were only inches apart, their chairs forming a perfectly equal triangle on the gray carpet.

The President smiled. His well-known weathered face and white hair were even more striking in person. "Brother Ellison, we've watched you and Sister Ellison for a number of years now. We know of your accomplishments, your devotion to the gospel, and your unfailing support of the leadership of the Church." President Wells paused. "We have something to suggest to you, and to Sister Wells," he said.

Grant wiped his damp hands together. He was nervous but excited. This has to be a call to be a General Authority, he thought. He had served as a bishop, a stake president, a mission president in Germany, and was now a full-time Regional Representative to England. Anna K. had served faithfully at his side, becoming a recognized leader in her own right. Right now she was serving on the Relief Society General Board, looking after it's interests in the British Isles. She had also become a well-known civic worker. Fluent in the major European languages, she was also a national director of the United Nation's Office of International Understanding, a position of considerable influence.

President Wells continued. "Sister Ellison, will you support your husband in any position we may call him to?"

Anna K. Ellison responded without hesitation. "Of course, President Wells." She sat erect in her chair, her smile serene and pleasant. Her hair was immaculate, her British clothes cut just right, and her hands rested calmly in her lap.

"Brother Ellison, will you support your wife in any position we may call her to?"

Ellison suddenly felt the pain in his left ankle. He rubbed it a little and said, "Why...ah...yes, of course, President."

"Well, I've got quite a proposal for you," President Wells said. "What I tell you now should not leave this room until it is announced in general conference next week. Last month, while in the temple, it was revealed to me that another person is to be called into the general leadership of the Church. I have discussed this call with the Twelve. They, too, have received a witness of what I propose to do." President Wells searched in his coat pocket for a sheet of paper. The old room was strangely quiet. Ellison leaned forward a little in his chair.

President Wells read carefully from the paper. "Anna K. Ellison, it is proposed that we call you to the position of Church Ambassador to Europe. This calling reports directly to the Twelve." President Wells paused and looked at Grant. "Brother Ellison, it is proposed that you be released from your present position as Regional Representative to support Sister Ellison. She's going to need your strength, your love, your experience, and your priesthood blessings."

Everyone exchanged glances. Anna K. Ellison, obviously concerned for her husband's feelings, looked to him. She instinctively knew how he was reacting and wondered how to handle the situation. Brother Ellison slumped slightly, and looked blankly at the President.

President Well's kind voice loosened the tight silence. "No need to answer just yet. You'll both need to think about it, I'm sure. Perhaps a little background information will help you understand the importance of this call."

President Wells leaned over to his to desk and touched a button. A side door opened and a handsome, well-dressed man appeared. "John, please bring us a pitcher of orange juice and have Lynn Maynard join us," the President said. Turning to the Ellisons, he continued, "Lynn is one of my personal assistants. I want you to understand how this call came about."

John returned with a tray containing cloth napkins, four crystal glasses and a large crystal pitcher of fresh orange juice. The President began to pour the juice.

Brother Ellison leaned back, folded his arms on his chest and choked down a cough. Lifting his left foot onto his right knee, he rubbed the tender ankle. His eyes wandered about the room, finally fixing on an early photograph of President Wells and his wife, Ellen Tanner Wells. She was clinging to his arm, looking lovingly into his face. That's the way things ought to be, Ellison thought. A woman at the side of her husband, supporting him.

Lynn Maynard, tall and stately, soon appeared with a large black binder. Sister Maynard was all business, and obviously well prepared for her presentation, which she supported with graphs and charts in the binder. "As you know," she began, "things have changed in the world, and in the Church, since the mid-eighties. In just twenty short years, we have sustained a growth of over 28 million new members, 10 million in Europe alone. "We've had a wonderful reception in Europe this past decade. And we've had a few problems, too. The Church's increased influence in Europe is being noticed by many ecclesiastical and government leaders, requiring our greater attention..." Lynn Maynard pushed smoothly through her prepared notes.

Ellison was not listening very closely. Why me, Heavenly Father? he prayed silently. He imagined himself following Anna into church and government buildings and being introduced as "Ambassador Ellison's husband." He saw himself addressing smiling Church members while they patiently waited for Anna K. Ellison to take the podium. He imagined waiting for her in hotel rooms while she attended important meetings, and then hearing her say, "I'm sorry, but what we discussed is confidential...I can't say anything just yet." He choked on that thought.

Where would his career go? It had been years since he had actively worked as an insurance executive. Now his career in the Church, whatever was left of it, would be overshadowed by Anna's position. He would have to defer to her needs, instead of her to his. His dream of rising to greater and greater service was about to turn into a nightmare—an uncontrollable plummeting into obscurity. He had a fleeting urge to jump up, flee the room, and quit the Church and his marriage. The sudden thought shook him like blue-sky thunder, and his attention flashed back to Sister Maynard.

"...And we've found the ambassadorship an excellent bridge to leaders around the world," Lynn Maynard continued. "It's opened many doors and helped us solve many problems. Ambassador Ellison will be the third ambassador called."

President Wells smiled and took Anna K. Ellison's hand. "They haven't accepted yet."

President Wells thanked Sister Maynard and invited her to chat for a moment with Sister Ellison. He stood and took Grant by the arm, moving him to the windows overlooking South Temple Street. Through the imperfect old glass Grant could see people passing three stories below, some intently heading for the temple, others for the mall, others seemingly with no destination in mind. None knew what was happening only feet above them.

"You're limping slightly," the President observed, turning back from the window to face Grant.

"It's a slight problem with my left ankle."

"I see. I hope it's only temporary. Brother Ellison, do you believe that God is making this call?" the President asked.

The question flashed on Grant's mind like water on a hot griddle. Do I? he wondered. "Yes, sir."

"My years of associating with people tell me you're having a problem, Brother Ellison. Am I right?"

Grant wanted to say, "No, I'm fine. I'd love to support Anna. I'm overjoyed at her call. I'll do whatever is required to see her succeed." Those feelings were there, all right, but they were swimming with a lot of other, more negative, selfish, and distrustful feelings. Grant knew how perceptive President Wells was. He would immediately feel of Grant's sincerity. Best to be completely honest, Grant told himself.

"Well, President Wells, it's not going to be easy, that's true. It's such a change. It's not that I don't want this for Anna, it's just that...well, pride is one of my problems...Anna can tell you. It's going to be rough being in the shadows...out of the decision making...not being 'number one'...not being in charge...taking direction from a woman...and from my wife, at that. I'm confused. I've been secretly hoping for something like this for myself for years...and now...it seems...I just don't know."

"Brother Ellison, thank you for being honest with me. This is hard on you, I can tell. You're not the first to experience these feelings, believe me," President Wells said with gentleness and love. "You saw the photo of Ellen and me on the desk. I keep that particular picture close to remind me that we are all equal in the sight of God, and that we must trust Him.

"That picture was taken on a Sunday afternoon many years ago. Ellen had just been called to a special committee of the Relief Society General Board, a tremendous opportunity, one requiring a lot of sacrifice on my part. I was then serving as the second counselor in an elders quorum presidency," he chuckled. "I felt some of the same hard emotions you are probably feeling right now—frustration, doubt, anger, rejection. And it took me months to overcome those feelings. But, it's my testimony that such feelings can be overcome and must be overcome if we are to achieve exaltation."

Grant nodded, not quite satisfied, not quite understanding, not quite believing. They walked back to the desk.

"Well, now, Sister Anna K. Ellison, will you accept this call from the Lord?"

"I will, with Grant's blessing."

"And you, Brother Grant R. Ellison, can you accept a new calling, that of supporting and sustaining Ambassador Anna K. Ellison?"

"I can try."

"Good. The Lord will help. I'd like you to join me as I set apart Sister Ellison. Then I'd like to lay my hands on your head and give you a special blessing, that you will be able to accept your new role, and to understand its importance to Anna and to yourself."

"Sister Ellison, if you'll come forward."

# Chapter 3

## Wonderful Wondering—
## Understanding Faith and Belief; Reason and Revelation

*Note: I gave the text of this address at a Regional Young Adult Fireside in 1983 and have since presented the material at least a dozen times in other settings and formats. My objectives are (1) to encourage more precise communications and intellectual honesty when dealing with religious questions and doubts, and (2) to describe differences between faith and belief, distrust and doubt, reason and revelation.*

It may help you to know that my calling in the Church is to sojourn with troubled people. Some call it lay counseling, although my mentor at LDS Social Services prefers "ministering." I am often immersed with people swimming against various emotional tides. Clear communication and honest understanding are two effective life preservers we use to reach calmer waters. Unfortunately, these two lifesavers seem out of reach—or unreal—for some Mormons struggling in the deep waters of our religion.

Many of us have difficulty communicating, both to ourselves and to others, about things that disturb us in our innermost and personal lives. And many of us are embarrassed or uneasy when listening to others with such problems. Many of you have had thoughts or questions like the following. Which would you feel free to verbalize publicly? Which have you heard others talking about openly?

— "Why would God command (Nephi to murder Laban, Joseph Smith to practice polygamy, Spencer Kimball to give priesthood to the blacks)?"
— "Is my (bishop, father, husband, stake president, leader) really inspired in this (decision, call, release, judgment)?"
— "The (Church, priesthood, bishop) treats me like (a child, a slave, a nobody.)"
— "I don't really know whether the (Church, prophet, gospel, Word of Wisdom) is true."

These are tough issues. Simply mentioning them causes some to react with uneasiness. Those among us who are unable to resolve such critical personal issues are likely either to drift into the lonely backwaters of closet doubting or to crawl out of the water onto the rocky shores of inactivity.

In thinking about this problem, I have come to the conclusion that our difficulty with communication and understanding stems partly from the blurred and imprecise usage of the most basic terms of the gospel—faith and belief—with their opposites distrust and doubt. We must also understand how they relate to knowledge and reason. Therefore, I want to explore the meanings of these terms with you and discuss how they may be used—and misused—in our personal lives.

## What are the Origins of Our Ideas? Our Beliefs?

Let's start by asking some fundamental questions:

What is the origin of an individual's ideas and beliefs and where does our knowledge begin? (1) Are these mental conditions born with us? (2) Do we get them only through sensory experiences? (3) Does God reveal them to us naturally (through natural means)? or supernaturally (through revelation or inspiration)?

I think if we opened up the discussion now, we'd find that most of us vaguely believe that all four sources contribute to our knowledge in varying degrees. Certainly, Mormon doctrine does not give us specific answers to these questions.

Ask yourself: Where did you get the idea that there is a God? Where did you get the belief that if you pray, God will provide an answer? How do you know the Church is true? Where did such beliefs and knowledge come from? Solid agreement and consistent answers would be highly improbable.

We might agree that everyone thinks. We think and form beliefs about the things around us. We make inferences from our experiences and draw conclusions which govern our actions. And our beliefs are often formed by what we want and what we need.

When the alarm clock rings, we have confidence that morning has arrived. (Yet I still look closely at the alarm clock, then at my watch—thus betraying an unconscious skeptism.) Inserting our key in the lock, we believe the door will open. In fact, our experience with keys is so successful that we "know" the door will open. Stepping on the brake will stop the car. We know it will. We put a lot of trust—a lot of faith—in those brakes. The point is, our lives are literally run by the beliefs developed through our sensory experiences.

But to what extent do beliefs and knowledge come from sources other than experience? And where does reason enter? In many early cultures, people unhesitatingly described the origin of their ideas as the spirits and gods which surrounded them at all times and in all places. Gods were the sources of good ideas and beliefs, devils the sources of wrong or wicked ideas.

Early Greek philosophers suggested that ideas and beliefs originate in sense perceptions and are refined and put to use through reason but that knowledge depended entirely upon the individual knower: "Your ideas and beliefs are yours, and mine are mine." Identical sense perception led to different, individual ideas and beliefs. For example, when we hear a Church leader talking about the need for more unquestioning obedience, it sounds very reasonable to some, suspect to others.

Socrates made great contributions to determining and acquiring beliefs and knowledge by developing a system of logical reasoning. Logic is either inductive (starting with facts and generalizing) or deductive (starting with a general principle and applying it to particulars.) Socrates' major contribution was his suggestion that sense perception is not an infallible approach to obtaining genuine, true knowledge. Our experience can deceive us.

Plato suggested that the soul came to the world already equipped with certain knowledge, a suggestion many of us today find harmonious with our belief in a premortal existence. The role of genetic factors and inherited knowledge is not clear.

During the early Christian era, Augustine added a third level. He taught that human beings received natural ideas through sense perception, and discovered others through reason but also received knowledge through revelation. Revealed knowledge was necessary for higher forms of living, granted as a gift through faith. This led to two levels of truth: that which was substantiated by perceptive, objective reasoning, and that which was substantiated by faith and the authority of the church.

For hundreds of years, this philosophy was used to protect faith in God and, in my opinion, misused to protect religious dogmas, particularly in cases of conflict between doctrines and rational, logical thinking. This approach allowed the dominant church to have a definition of knowledge that extended far beyond that of sense perception and direct, logical experience. When people reached the limits of logically-derived knowledge, they were able to accept the doctrines of the church through the *divine* method of knowledge generation. And it was commonly assumed that divine knowledge was superior to sense- and reason-derived knowledge. (Although I've described these levels as progressing from lower to higher, it is more likely that they co-existed simultaneously, with different realms for their domain. For example, sensory experience would easily teach a family that the Black Death could kill, and reason would urge them to avoid those who were already plague victims, but "divine" Knowledge, as authoritatively pronounced by ecclesiastical leaders, would identify the origin of the plague, not as rat-borne microbes, but as God's displeasure with human sin.)

Thus, it is easy to see how the church, in addition to supplying answers to ultimate questions about the purpose of life, found itself correcting reason when ideas and beliefs generated through experience, study, and thinking contradicted religious authority. The well-known story of Galileo demonstrates the church's power suppress natural knowledge (a solar system with the sun at its center) to protect "revealed" knowledge (that the earth on which Adam and Eve were created constituted the center of God's creations).

Contradictions of authoritarian knowledge did, in fact, bring charges of heresy which lead to excommunication, banishment, and even death in some cases; but despite imbalances of power, revealed Knowledge and knowledge based on observation and experimentation, the foundation of today's scientific method, have never been able to supplant each other completely.

Today, as at the beginning of recorded history, religion does not supply certain answer about the specific origins, use, or development of ideas, beliefs, and knowledge. Modern science, however, has adopted an almost total reliance on inductive reasoning based upon experimentation, observation, and testing. If a phenomenon cannot be studied by this method, it is usually excluded as a proper subject for scientific inquiry. This reliance has been felt strongly in our culture during the past eighty-five years. Indeed it has affected every facet of life, including religion. We expect proof; we are skeptical; we tend to disbelieve any claim made without evidence. How many TV advertisements can you believe, for example? Those who habitually believe are called "gullible."

Most importantly, the scientific era has produced new terms like *statistical confidence* and *normal distribution*, and has created new meanings for old terms like *belief*, *knowledge*, *doubt*, *faith*, and *reason*.

## Defining our Terms

Now we return to the problem I introduced at the beginning. Many of us haven't yet come to terms with the confused and overlapping meanings assigned by science and religion to the same words. Little wonder we have trouble communicating!

### *To believe*

When I say *belief*, I mean *personal belief*. I will not be referring to belief as a creed, as a list of doctrines, or as a particular church or religious group.

Henry Eyring, probably the best-known Mormon scientist, made an interesting observation about personal belief: "In this Church we don't have to believe anything that isn't true." This is a wonderful statement, but we need to be careful in our definitions of "believe" and "true." If we don't, we invite trouble into our lives.

In its modern, science-influenced sense, *to believe* is to accept or conclude something from a solid data base. For example, if we flip a coin fifty times and tabulate the results of heads versus tails, we are likely to believe from the evidence that each comes up about equally, although we can't guarantee anything on a single trial.

Personal belief, in this narrow sense, implies a conscious mental acceptance of something as true based on reason, experience, information, evidence, prejudice, or the authority of the thing's source. Unfortunately, as the Greeks suggested, each person's interpretation of the evidence will vary:

- A mother looks at a newborn baby and sees evidence of the existence of God. A biochemist looks at a newborn baby and marvels at the power of evolution.

- A poet looks at a law-abiding universe as sufficient evidence to prove the existence of a creator. An astronomer looks at the universe and believes it to be only a great ordered randomness.

- One university student says her education caused her to lose her religious beliefs; another says an identical education has strengthened her.

- One person believes in Joseph Smith because of the authority of those who claim his prophethood; another rejects Joseph Smith on the authority of those who deny his work.

Personal beliefs can be modified, verified, strengthened, weakened, and tested by the day-to-day experiences and information supplied to the mind. The strength of beliefs can be measured. Figure 1 lets you test your beliefs. The scale is calibrated from 0 to 10; 5 represents no belief, opinion, or knowledge, 10 represents positive knowledge ("I know it is correct."), and 0 represents negative knowledge ("I know it is not correct.") Numbers inbetween represent strengths of belief or doubt. Where does your belief fall for each statement?

**FIGURE 1. Tests of Intellectual Belief**

| | | Increasing Doubt | | | No Opinion No Belief | | | Increasing Belief | | |
|---|---|---|---|---|---|---|---|---|---|---|
| 0 | 1 | 2 | 3 | 4 | 5 | 6 | 7 | 8 | 9 | 10 |

1. ____ Six divided by zero is zero.
2. ____ The integral of 2 is 2X.
3. ____ Joseph Smith lived.
4. ____ Joseph Smith was a prophet.
5. ____ Joseph Smith's death was part of God's plan.

(Answers. 1. False. The answer is infinity. 2. True, according to the rules of integral calculus. 3. The evidence is great that he lived. 4. Your choice. 5. Ditto.)

There are four lessons to be learned from this quiz. First, belief is not necessarily perfect knowledge. (Were all of your answers "10"?) Second, one may not have sufficient experience or information to have any belief, or at best, have only weak belief. (Could you answer Question 2?). Third, one's beliefs may be in error. (Was your answer to Question 1 correct?) And four, not everyone's answers are the same. (Would your mother's answer to Question 5 be the same as yours?) A more detailed self-assessment instrument appears in Chapter 4, "Personal Beliefs and Church Activity."

How often are our beliefs inaccurate? Unfortunately, more than we might like to admit. At one time the earth was thought to be flat. It looks flat. Our senses tell us it is flat. There are still people who claim to believe in a flat earth. But is it? A stick in water appears bent. We know from the laws of refraction why it seems bent. But at one time in our human history much effort was made to explain the bending, all futile because the basic belief was in error.

## *To have faith*

Note that the word *faith* has not yet entered into our discussion.

Faith has many meanings, and again, I want to look at a narrow definition related to personal faith. I will not be using faith as a religion, faith as honesty, faith as being staunch, or faith as a religious community, as in "the faithful."

"Having faith" in something—for example, having a personal faith in the Book of Mormon—implies making a bridge between what we know, or believe, about the book and what the book claims to be. Faith implies a willingness to follow the book's teachings, assent, and acceptance.

Righteousness and the ability to have faith seem to be related. Job, a righteous man and perhaps the most faithful of all men says, "Though He slay me, yet will I trust in him" (Job 13:15). Peter says, quoting Habakkuk, "The just shall live by faith." (Rom. 1:17)

I have a personal belief that faith is a gift from God. I reason that it comes as the result of prayer and fasting. It may be earned. It may wax and wane as a function of righteousness. Faith may come through inspiration and revelation. I may be wrong, but I believe God's answer to a request for knowledge may often be given as the strength to have faith.

Note that I have said I *believe* these things about faith. My thoughts about faith can be changed and expanded upon. On the belief scale of Figure 1, I would place my personal beliefs about faith at about "8".

There is no stigma attached to simply believing, and conversely, no disgrace attached to saying "I don't know for sure."

### *Faith and belief*

Faith and belief are often regarded in religion and philosophy as synonymous. Most dictionaries define one by the other. The scriptures often use them interchangeably. However, let us borrow from the rational vocabulary of science to make a distinction between the two that I think is useful.

Belief implies intellectual assent, while *faith* implies confidence, trust, and conviction. Belief is passive--an agreement with or acceptance of an existing proposition when it is offered. Faith is active--a reliance and trust which impels one to action. Belief is a product of the mind, faith a product of the heart.

In Matthew 17:18-21, Christ tells the apostles why they were unable to cast out a devil. The sixteenth-century King James version reads: "And Jesus said unto them, Because of your unbelief; for verily I say unto you, If ye have faith as a grain of mustard seed, ye shall say unto this mountain, remove...."

However, the twentieth-century Revised Standard Version reads: "He said to them, 'Because of your little faith. For truly, I say to you, if you have faith as a grain of mustard seed, you will say to this mountain....'"

Notice that "unbelief" becomes "little faith" in the modern translation. There is an interesting problem related to the word *faith:* it has no verb form. There are verbs for belief, trust, doubt, knowledge, and reason, that is to believe, to trust, to doubt, to know, to reason. If we need to express faith as action, as a verb, we must use other words: "I believe," or "I accept", or "I trust," or "I have faith in...."

Doctrine and Covenants 49:12 contains the commandment: "Believe in the name of the Lord Jesus." Ordering someone to believe is like commanding someone to understand. Can it be done simply as an act of will? Usually not. The commandment seems irrational unless we see the verb "to believe" as synonymous with active faith. God can, if fact, command us to "be faithful." But if we interpret belief as faith, we should not confuse the opposite of belief (doubt) with the opposite of faith (distrust, nihilism).

When an emotionally distraught person says, "I doubt (and I feel guilty about doubting)," we talk about living by faith. Doubt and faith go together like hunger and food. Hunger drives the search for food and doubt can drive the search for new understanding.

## *To doubt*

Doubt, in the modern sense, means to be unsettled in belief or opinion, to be uncertain or undecided. It means not having sufficient information or evidence upon which to build belief, or having negative evidence. Suppose a scientist administers a particular dose of promising medicine to six diseased rats. They all die. The scientist must conclude that there is not enough evidence to justify belief that the medicine can be effective. Additional trials with other dosages will be necessary before conclusions can be drawn.

The older, religious meanings for doubt are *distrust*, and *to reject*. We are commanded to "doubt not." In its broad, historical sense, doubt is associated with the most negative of human traits—the absence of trust in God and the rejection of his existence and goodness. Little wonder that doubt still has such a strong negative connotation, even today when skepticism and questioning are taught as highly desirable consumer skills.

Almost every Mormon is prey to religious uncertainties, questions, and doubts of varying intensities. Free agency requires us to make continual choices. The veil ensures that we will never have complete information to be certain that any given choice is correct. A person who fails to tune into his/her awareness, and who represses the natural urge to question to maintain an image of absolute certainty may settle for the appearance of being a believer rather than for its actuality. In those unable to acknowledge and manage doubts, individual conscience and the weight of authority join battle. Eventually, one or the other must be denied for the sake of emotional stability. Unfortunately, the denial of either is not desireable. Denial of conscience creates unthinking robots. Denial of authority results in inactivity and the loss of blessings.

## *To Question*

Questioning is the delightful offspring of doubting. Having questions implies a desire to expand the data base upon which beliefs are built. Questions represent the opportunity to exercise faith.

Unfortunately, questioning is often considered to be a negative activity. Suppose, for example, an elders quorum is studying 1 Nephi, and one man questions the standard interpretation of why Nephi is justified in killing Laben. It just doesn't seem to fit the gospel as he understands it. Why would the Lord would command one man to kill another? he wonders. How does he seek information and express his true feelings without sounding distrustful, negative, or non-supportive? Which of the following honest statements would not sound threatening in some priesthood classes?

"I am skeptical of..."
"I doubt..."
"I can't believe that..."
"I don't believe that..."
"My mind says it couldn't be true that..."
"I have a real question about the interpretation..."
"My understanding of the gospel makes it difficult for me to believe that..."

Such statements might be interpreted by others in the quorum as betrayal, faithlessness, slothfulness, contentiousness, and not being one with the Brethren (General Authorities). Such unfortunate interpretations are, however, cultural. They were learned. They can be unlearned.

### *To know*

In a modern, personal, and intellectual sense "to know" is to have a clear understanding, to be relatively sure, to gain intellectual understanding as a result of study, experience, reasoning, or evidence. *Knowledge* is familiarity with, or awareness of, facts and evidence. But in this life nothing can be known with perfection, only with degrees of confidence. Neither science nor earthly religion claims perfect knowledge. Thus, all knowledge is not without reservation. For example, at three o'clock I believe the mail has arrived because it usually comes by then; I am more sure when I look out the window and see an envelope in the mailbox; I know it is there when I go to the box and grasp the envelope; but I am dismayed when I see that the envelope is a flyer put there by the corner gas station. Now I believe the mail is late; I am again surprised to learn that my daughter actually retrieved the mail at two o'clock, and that it is on my desk.

We approach perfect knowledge asymtotically. Science and statistics have developed elaborate methods for testing, verifying, and strengthening the evidence upon which beliefs and knowledge are based. But no test produces perfect knowledge. For example, to determine the toxicity of a chemical, studies may be conducted with mice. Varying amounts of the chemical may be injected to determine the LD-50 (the lethal dose for 50 percent of the mouse sample.) The results suggest the toxicity of the chemical, but few would claim perfect knowledge. In this modern sense, *knowledge* can be thought of as near-perfect or almost infinite belief.

But again, in traditional and religious usage, knowing and knowledge have meanings related to belief. Testimonies often contain statements of "knowing." This type of knowing has its origins in feelings, emotions, and metaphysical experiences—sources of evidence not generally acceptable to measurement and verification. At some point belief becomes strong enough to be thought of as knowledge. For example, suppose you enter a room, find the light switch, and flip the switch several times. If the light always comes on, we assume to "know" it will always come on. (I am always startled by a burned-out bulb.)

Another source of "knowledge" is the voice of authority. The missionaries, our teachers, or our parents may have told us that God would answer our prayers. The authority of the source was strong enough for us to believe that it could happen. When we prayed, most of us received additional evidence, however subjective, of the truth of the claim. Many of us "know" by this method that God answers prayer.

For some, a little evidence is sufficient to graduate a "belief" to "knowledge." For others a great deal of evidence is required. Suppose a person is phoning a friend. After three rings one person may hang up, "knowing" that the friend is out. Another person may wait ten rings before hanging up. Still another may wait twenty rings "to be sure." Still, we can never have absolute knowledge that the friend was not home. Perhaps he or she was in the shower. Perhaps the friend would have picked up the phone on the twenty-first ring.

We all "know" that Joseph Smith lived. At least we're pretty sure. No one living today has seen him but the circumstantial evidence is excellent. Our confidence in that "knowledge" is high. But was he a prophet? Did God appear to him? Here there is evidence, too. But most of us must be satisfied with subjective evidence—inspiration, feelings, emotions. Our answers to those questions involve faith, making inevitable the emergence of doubts and questions.

### Summary

I have discussed past and present meanings of the words *faith*, *belief*, *doubt*, *knowledge*, and *reason*, pointing out that it is possible to define each quite precisely. I have talked about natural and supernatural sources of information and the uncertainty associated with both. Finally, I have suggested that precise communication and understanding is both desirable and possible.

Many of us have religious questions and doubts, but they do not mean we distrust God or reject his goodness in our lives. It is okay to have questions. It is okay to ask them.

What can we do when we have questions about our religion? If we wonder? If we doubt certain aspects of the gospel? The modern answer is to increase the evidence, to build a stronger data base upon which to believe. (The evidence may be either temporal or spiritual.) This means studying, praying, and working for it. But this is fun and exciting! It makes life fuller. It adds the strength of intelligence to the power of our feelings.

In the meantime, while the evidence is building, we must rely on faith to bridge the gap. I pray the Lord will help us find the evidence. . . but also provide us that magnificent bridge.

# Chapter 4

## Personal Beliefs and Church Activity—A Self-Assessment

In the early 1980's, the Church (through its Correlation Department) conducted an extensive survey among Mormons called the *Survey of Religion and Life.* This lengthy survey probed many facets of Mormon life, including levels of belief and activity. The results have not been published, as far as I know, but I was given the opportunity to see some of the results related to personal belief and activity.

I have prepared a similar, but much abbreviated questionnaire. I think you will find it fun and informative.

A word of caution: things in print take on a validity that may not be warranted. I've used this survey informally at firesides, in Sunday school classes, etc., and people seem to think it gives accurate information. However it has not been scientifically developed or tested. It may not function well for the elderly, teenagers, the infirm or handicapped, the ill, the poor, or for those not living in close proximity to an active Mormon community—in other words, for those who do not share most of the characteristics of a mainstream Mormon.

This self-administered questionnaire is intended to probe your personal beliefs and compare them to your Church activity. To understand the terms I am using, please read the essay on page 15, "Wonderful Wondering," Chapter 3. The questionnaire asks you to share private feelings and thoughts. It touches on items that are normally confidential and sensitive. You will need to be thoughtful and honest as you answer each question.

## Section One
## Measures of Participation and Activity in Standard Church Programs

1. How often do you attend the temple?

(Use this first set if you live near a temple, e.g., within a two-hour drive.)

0 ( ) No temple recommend; no attendance in one year
1 ( ) Once per year
2 ( ) 2-3 times per year
3 ( ) 4-6 times per year
4 ( ) 7-10 times per year
5 ( ) Once per month, or more

(Use this set if you live far from a temple, e.g., more than a two-hour drive.)

0 ( ) No temple recommend
1 ( ) None
2 ( ) Once per year
3 ( ) Once or twice per year
4 ( ) Two times per year
5 ( ) Three or more times per year

2. How much of the Word of Wisdom do you follow?

0 ( ) I ignore the Word of Wisdom
1 ( ) Not very much
2 ( ) I abstain from alcohol and tobacco, most of the time
3 ( ) I abstain from alcohol, tobacco, coffee and tea;
almost all the time
4 ( ) All of above, all the time
5 ( ) All of above plus caffeine drinks, chocolate, meat in winter

3. When you receive (or, if you should receive) a church calling from your bishop, you:

0 ( ) Never accept
1 ( ) Rarely accept
2 ( ) Accept only if convenient and desirable for me
3 ( ) Accept if certain conditions are met
4 ( ) Accept after discussion and prayer
5 ( ) Always accept without question

4. Describe your attendance at regular meetings (e.g., Sunday School, priesthood meeting, or Relief Society, sacrament meeting, Mutual, as applicable.)

0 ( ) Never attend
1 ( ) Rarely attend
2 ( ) Occasionally (less than 40%)
3 ( ) Quite often (40-75%)
4 ( ) Regularly (more than 75%)
5 ( ) Never miss any meetings

5. During an average week, how many hours do you spend in church-related activities? (Attendance at all meetings, socials, lesson preparation, home/visiting teaching, temple work, etc.)

0 ( ) 0
1 ( ) 1
2 ( ) 2-3
3 ( ) 4-5
4 ( ) 6-7
5 ( ) 8 or more

6. Describe your actual donations to the Church during the past several years.

0 ( ) No donations to Church
1 ( ) Irregular donations only, and only if asked
2 ( ) Occasional donations
3 ( ) Part tithe payer plus occasional other donations
4 ( ) Usually full tithe payer plus other offerings
5 ( ) Full tithe payer plus all other offerings

## Scoring

The above questions are a rough measure of your activity and participation in traditional church programs.

Count the scores based on your answers. The following results are not definitive but suggest trends:

| | |
|---|---|
| 22-30 | Very active; high participation |
| 15-21 | Moderately active |
| 7-14 | Moderately inactive |
| 0-6 | Very inactive; little participation |

We will use these results in Section Three. If you scored 15 or higher, consider yourself "Active." If you scored 14 or less, consider yourself "Inactive."

## Section Two
## Measures of Belief

In this section we ask you to describe your real, personal thoughts and conclusions about the statements shown below. Answer honestly, not as you think you should.

Zero represents negative knowledge—"I know the statement isn't correct; I know it isn't true." Numbers four to one represent increasing doubt—"I don't know for sure, but I doubt it is incorrect; I don't think the statement is true."

Number five represents lack of information and lack of belief one way or the other—"I don't know; I have no opinion; I have no thoughts one way or the other."

Ten represents positive knowledge—"I know the statement is correct; I know it is true beyond any doubt." Numbers between six and nine represent increasingly strong belief—"I don't know for sure, but I believe the statement is true;" "I think it is correct."

| <---- Stronger Doubt | | | | No Opinion, No Information | | | Stronger Belief ----> | | | |
|---|---|---|---|---|---|---|---|---|---|---|
| 0 | 1 | 2 | 3 | 4 | 5 | 6 | 7 | 8 | 9 | 10 |

Examples--

( 10 ) Two plus two equals four.
( 3 ) A Democrat will be elected president in the next election.
( 5 ) James Quentin Smith is a parliamentarian in New Zealand.

## A. Beliefs about the Church and its Unique Doctrines

The following statements represent common doctrines and teachings which set Mormonism apart from other religious creeds and organizations. Please indicate your level of belief in the following statements. (Remember, record what you truly think, not what you're supposed to think and not what you are willing to accept by faith.)

1. ( ) The Mormon Church is the one and only true church.

2. ( ) All other religious sects are wrong, their creeds are an abomination, and their professors are all corrupt in the sight of God.

3. ( ) God and Jesus came to a grove of trees in which Joseph Smith was praying.

4. ( ) The Book of Mormon was translated from gold plates which an angel gave Joseph.

5. ( ) Joseph Smith translated the Book of Abraham directly from Egyptian papyri upon which Abraham himself had made a record.

6. ( ) God inspired Joseph Smith to practice polygamy.

7. ( ) The temple ceremony was written under the direction and inspiration of God and contains his thoughts and desires.

8. ( ) Christ's gospel is being correctly represented by the Church.

9. ( ) Your bishop was called under the inspiration of God.

10. ( ) It is important to gain a testimony that Joseph Smith was a true and faithful prophet.

The above statements attempt to measure your personal beliefs about the Church's unique teachings and doctrines.

Score your answers as follows:

| | | |
|---|---|---|
| 75-100 points | — | Strong belief and acceptance of Church's unique teachings |
| 50-75 | — | Moderate belief and acceptance |
| 25-49 | — | More doubt than belief |
| 0-25 | — | Serious doubts of the Church's unique teachings |

We will be using these results in Section Three. Count yourself a "Believer in Unique Church Teachings" if you scored 50-100 points. Count yourself a "Disbeliever in Unique Church Teachings" if you scored less than 50 points.

### B. Beliefs About Your Personal Relationship to God and Your Feelings about Christ's Teachings

This section tries to measure your thoughts and conclusions about your relationship to God and about your personal beliefs about Jesus Christ and his teachings.

Please rank your beliefs, as above. (Remember to record what you truly think, not what you're supposed to believe, or what you are willing to accept on faith.)

1. ( ) I am inspired by God.
2. ( ) I usually receive answers to prayer, directly or indirectly.
3. ( ) I am able to communicate with God.
4. ( ) I'm happy as a Christian.
5. ( ) I have been personally blessed by God.
6. ( ) I feel close to God; I feel that Christ is my brother.
7. ( ) I read from the New Testament often.
8. ( ) Christ's teachings are the most important thing in my life.
9. ( ) It is important to gain a testimony that Christ is the Savior of

the world.

10. ( ) Christ's teachings are the most true religious teachings on the earth at this time.

The above statements attempt to measure your personal beliefs about your relationship to God and Jesus Christ, and your thoughts about Christ's teachings in your life.

Score your answers as follows:

| | |
|---|---|
| 81-100 points | — Strong personal beliefs in God and Jesus Christ; positive relationship with God. |
| 50-80 | — Moderate personal belief in God and Jesus Christ; a developing relationship with God. |
| 21-49 | — Moderate personal disbelief in God and Jesus Christ; weak personal relationship with God. |
| 0-20 | — Serious doubts about God, Jesus Christ, and His teachings; little personal relationship with God. |

In Section Three we will be using these results. Please count yourself a "Personal Believer in God and Jesus" if you scored 50-100 points in this part of Section Two. Count yourself a "Personal Disbeliever in God and Jesus" if you scored less than 50 points.

## Section Three
## Results and Discussion.

Based on the above exercises, you will find yourself in one each of the following sections. (Check one box in each section.)

### Section One.

| | |
|---|---|
| Active | [ ] |
| Inactive | [ ] |

### Section Two-A

| | |
|---|---|
| Believer in unique church teachings | [ ] |
| Disbeliver in unique church teachings | [ ] |

## Section Two-B

Personal believer in God and Jesus [ ]
Personal disbeliever in God and Jesus [ ]

The accompanying figure shows three 2x2 matrices. Note that your results in the above three sections will place you in one of the squares in each matrix. For example, if you were "Active" in Section One, a "believer in Unique Church Teachings" Section Two-A, and a "personal believer in God and Jesus," you would place your self in blocks 1, 5, and 9.

Check the blocks which pertain to you.

| | Active | Inactive |
|---|---|---|
| Believer in Unique Church Teachings | 1 | 2 |
| Disbeliever in Unique Church Teachings | 3 | 4 |

| | Active | Inactive |
|---|---|---|
| Personal Believer in God and Jesus | 5 | 6 |
| Personal Disbeliever in God and Jesus | 7 | 8 |

| | Believer in Unique Church Teachings | Disbeliever in Unique Church Teachings |
|---|---|---|
| Personal Believer in God and Jesus | 9 | 10 |
| Personal Disbeliever in God and Jesus | 11 | 12 |

## DISCUSSION

As you have experienced, it is difficult to measure something as complex as personal belief. It is certainly difficult to interpret any such results accurately. Therefore, you should take the following interpretations (and any personal conclusions) with a grain of salt. If the outcome disturbs you, you might want to discuss it with your Bishop.

| Mark in Block | Possible Interpretation |
|---|---|
| 1. | This block represents both positive beliefs and activity in the Church, the predominant situation found among active Mormons. |
| 2. | This block indicates a belief in Church claims but little activity in Church programs. A person in this block does not have the level of activity of others with similar beliefs. There could be any number of reasons: poor health, estrangement, feelings of rejection, hurt feelings, habit, habitual sin, and so forth. I would expect some people in this block to be suffering emotional trauma because of the apparent conflict in beliefs and actions. |
| 3. | A mark in this block indicates activity, but disbelief in the Church and its unique teachings. This person falls into a group known as "active doubters," "faithful doubters," or "closet doubters." The study mentioned at the beginning of this article (conducted by the Church Correlation Department) suggested that some active Mormons may fall in this category. Such persons remain active for a number of reasons, some of which are described in the essay, "The Phenomenon of the Closet Doubter." See Chapter 1. |
| 4. | This block indicates weak activity and disbelief in Church teachings, a condition we would not find unusual among inactive and former Mormons. |
| 5. | This block represents both positive beliefs in Jesus and God, and activity in the Church, again, the predominant situation found among most active Mormons. |
| 6. | This block indicates a belief in God and Jesus but little activity in Church programs. A person in this block might have rejected the Church, or might be inactive for any number of reasons. |

7. A mark in this block indicates activity, but disbelief in God and Jesus. Again, this person may fall into the group known as "active doubters."

8. This block indicates weak activity and disbelief in God and Jesus, a condition we would not find unusual among inactive and former Mormons.

9. This block represents a person who believes in the Church and has positive personal beliefs in and ties to God and Jesus Christ. Again, this would be a common occurrence among active Mormons.

10. This block presents an anomaly (at least for Mormons): the person believes in God and Jesus, but disbelieves unique Church teachings. This person has accepted God and Jesus, but does not accept claims of the Church.

11. This block represents another anomoly, that of belief in the Church and its teachings but a lack of personal belief in God and Jesus. This person might be caught up in the organization and programs of the Church, but has not yet developed a personal religion.

12. This block represents persons who disbelieve both the Church and Christ, and who have not developed a personal relationship with God. This would probably be common among inactive or former Mormons who have rejected both the Church and Christ.

As I have administered this questionnaire to members at firesides, quorum meetings, etc., I have observed mostly positive levels of both belief and activity among those who participated—with exceptions, of course. And, I have noticed the ever-present problem of word definition. Many people simply cannot separate faith and intellectual belief. This works to the benefit of some (those who live by faith) and to the detriment of others (those who see lack of belief as lack of faith.)

Remember, the self-assessment is intended to compare intellectual beliefs with activity, not faithfulness with activity.

# Chapter 5

# The Gift

*The most pernicious of absurdities is that...blind faith is better that the constant practice of every human virtue.* -- Walter Savage Landor

*In some circles of the Church, much is made of heavenly gifts--the power to heal or to speak in tongues, the gift of a sure knowledge--and the faith required to make them viable. Modern scriptures tell us that many will be given such gifts.*

*Responses to heaven-sent gifts vary with the person. Most of those blessed with gifts exercise them with humility, while others feel a measure of pride. Some who lack such gifts simply deny their existence, others feel guilty that they have no gifts, and still others think they may not be worthy to exercise their gift. Many Mormons measure their faith by their ability to exercise gifts of the Spirit.*

*Healing--the laying of hands to cure illness--is one gift that touches almost every Mormon regularly. This story describes one man's response to his gift.*

John carefully guided the big car out of the Cottonwood Hospital parking lot. He smiled slightly and lifted his hand to the top of the wheel. Balding, middle-aged, short and portly, John was known as "the Baptist" in his ward because of his zeal for missionary work.

He, the bishop, and Dan, the other counselor, were silent as they headed for the freeway. The sky was darkening in the early evening, the air biting and heavy with winter moisture. It seemed like a long time before anyone spoke.

"I hope Sister Fuller heard the blessing you gave her, John," Dan said from the back seat.

"I'm sure she did, Dan. She had her eyes open and I saw a little glistening moisture." John unbuttoned his coat and loosened his tie. The car heater was beginning to do its job.

"Well, it was beautiful. You did a wonderful job in there," the bishop said firmly. Turning, he said, "You okay back there, Dan?" He loosened his seat belt. He was at least six inches taller than either John or Dan and would have preferred to sit in the back—just a part of his habitual helpfulness. But with advancing age and arthritis, he was finding the back seats of cars uncomfortable. Even his office chair was a torture when he sat more than an hour at a time.

"Thanks, I'm fine," Dan responded. Muscular, red hair, high-school eduction, railroad fireman, Dan had just turned thirty. Teenagers liked him for his humor, selfless attitude, and impressive athletic abilities.

Freeway silence filled the old Lincoln sedan as they headed north. Smaller cars whooshed by. John didn't care about his speed. He was preoccupied with the afterglow of the blessing. Healing was his spiritual gift. Many times he had felt an unseen influence telling him what to say during the sealing prayer. Anointing was okay, but sealing gave him a chance to say those wonderful things that entered into his mind. Put there by the Spirit, he reminded himself. "Healings are just one of the many powers of the priesthood," he announced aloud, hoping to re-establish some sense of humility. He kept his gaze to the front.

A small man, John felt like a John Wayne on these occasions. The power to heal—the gift to make things better—this was divine reassurance. It means that God trusts me, right? Would he allow me to be filled with the power to heal otherwise? Of course not, John thought.

The lights of the interchange swept past. They turned west off the freeway. The road got suddenly dark. Distant lights flickered with loneliness on the Oquirrhs. Memories and faces flooded his mind: Charles Devereau, in France, during his mission, an epileptic. John had offered him a blessing—there had been no request. After the blessing, Charles cried and grabbed John's hands, and wouldn't let go. An emotional scene followed for about ten minutes. As far as John knew, Charles had never had another epileptic attack. There was Joyce Smith, his cousin, who was stung by a bee and almost died. And Sister Sorenson's fever. Dan's broken foot. The faces and names popped up and passed like lines on the road.

Dan broke the silence. "John, you really have a gift for blessing people. I don't ever recall being at ease when I've been called upon to give the sealing. How do you do it?"

John shifted slightly in his seat, responding seriously. "The D&C tells us that some people are given special gifts. You know, some people speak in tonques, some can preach with power. I seem to be able to heal people. It's nothing I earned or asked for. It just seems to be my gift, I guess. 'Course, I've worked to develop the faith to exercise the gift. If you don't exercise it, you'll lose it."

John glanced at Dan's face in the rear-view mirror. After several seconds Dan said, with a hint of remorse and guilt in his voice, "I guess I've tried to cover my nervousness...or lack of faith, maybe...by using the sealing to calm or to comfort. I always end up saying something positive, but vague, like, 'We know the Lord loves you.' Or, 'He will be by your side. He will do what is right for you. He knows your needs.' Stuff like that. People seem relieved and happy for the blessing. I always feel guilty, though."

John wanted not to sound judgmental. "I guess the people I feel sorry for are those who always say, 'You will be healed, *if* it is the Lord's will,' or, '*if* you have faith.' Those are cop-outs that rob the sick person of a true priesthood blessing." He gripped the steering wheel a little harder.

The bishop turned and spoke to Dan, "Healings are like any spiritual experience. These things work by faith. And, you've got to be worthy to make things happen."

John focused on the windshield. He smiled to himself. The thought repeated itself in his mind: "You've got to be worthy."

John was shaving when the bishop phoned the next morning. "What's the matter?" he asked with a husky morning voice.

"I just got a call from the hospital," the bishop said slowly. "Sister Fuller passed away during the night."

"Oh, no..." John took the phone to the bed and sat down. "How? What in the world happened?"

"I don't know, for sure. The nurse just said she died during the night. They found her this morning. They think it might have been a ruptured blood vessel. The doctor feels she died quickly and with little more than a fleeting moment of final awareness or pain."

"Ahh . . .mmmm . . . thanks for calling me. Oh, ahh, when's the funeral going to be?" John asked, his voice weak.

"Day after tomorrow. I'll need you there for support, okay?"

During the funeral, John sat next to the bishop. The funeral was typically Mormon--fond farewell with hope and promise. Following the service, the bishopric met in the Bishop's office.

"John, you're awfully quiet today. I didn't know that you were that close to Sister Fuller," the Bishop said, trying to ease John's anguish.

"Well, we were closer than most people thought," John responded, emptily. After a pause, he said, "Bishop, look, I'm really . . . ahh . . . thinking about the blessing I gave Sister Fuller. You, her husband, the nurses, Dan . . . . What must you all be thinking? What happened? Why did I say what I said? Why did she die after a priesthood blessing? What happened to the gift?"

The Bishop said, "John, who really knows the ways of the Lord? Who really understands the mysteries of faith and heavenly gifts?" He threw his arms up in a gesture of perplexity. He stood and came close, his hand on John's shoulder. "I don't have any judgements to make about the blessing, John. You'll be carrying the experience with you, though. You'll have to live with it, and think about it, and pray about it."

John sat quietly, not sure what to say. The Bishop reached down and took John's hand. "Come on, lets go be with Brother Fuller and his family. We still have the gift of love to share--and there's no question about how it works."

John nodded.

# Chapter 6

## Adam and Eve: The Dawn of Consciousness and The Birth of Faith

(A one-act play in three scenes)

*The only good is knowledge, the only evil, ignorance.* -- Socrates

*How calmly may we commit ourselves into the hands of Him who bears up the world.* -- Jean Paul Richter

*Note: The great themes of Genesis (the creation, the fall, the eventual victory of life over death, the relationship of man and woman, knowledge of good and evil, the need for faith, the role of the adversary, the love of God, agency, and obedience) are universal concerns. They appear again and again in scripture, drama, art, music, and literature. The appearance of a familiar theme in yet another verse, play, picture, or song does not necessarily distract or invalidate previous expressions of the theme. Rather, new ways of expressing the ideas and ideals of a great theme help us visualize and put into perspective the many facets of the theme.*

Cast of characters in order of appearance:

Narrator
God-the-Father
Jehovah, the Son of God
Michael the Archangel (Adam)
Eve
Satan
Seth, a son of Adam and Eve
Two other adults, children of Adam and Eve

## Scene 1. THE DAWN OF CREATION

NARRATOR: In the beginning, God commanded Jehovah and Michael to organize a world in six great creative periods. In obedience they ventured into the void and through discipline caused the sun, the moon, and the stars to appear. Through love they formed mountains and seas, deserts and streams, fishes and fowl. In joy they gave variety and beauty to the face of the earth. We now join them during the final day of creation: "And the Lord God formed man of the dust of the ground, and breathed into his nostrils the breath of life; and man became a living soul" *(Gen. 2:7).*

*(Lights up on God, Jehovah, and Michael, center stage; lighting as if at dawn, in a garden.)*

GOD *(majestic, loving):* My son, see the earth which arises in splendor, there is no one to care for it. Let us form man in our own likeness; and in our own image let us form woman.

JEHOVAH (*dignified, loving*): Behold Michael. When he awakens, he will have become Adam; and having forgotten everything, will be

naive. *(Contemplative)* Father, is it good for a man to be alone?

GOD: To stand alone is to know melancholy. To lie alone is to know desolation. From his bone we shall create bone, from his flesh, flesh.

*(Eve appears from behind Adam.)*

JEHOVAH: Adam, awake! We have created this woman to be a companion for you; and you to be a companion for her.

GOD: Adam, behold Eve. She is the mother of all living, the matriarch of all learning; she is the beginning of love.

ADAM: She is as sweet as a spring flower.

JEHOVAH: We have planted this garden eastward in Eden, at a place to be known forever as Adam-ondi-aman; and here you may live in perfect contentment.

*(Lights dim momentarily, then come up again, a later day in the Garden of Eden.)*

*Note: Because characterization through dialoque is sparse, action and movement must carry this aspect. Adam and Eve should be shown as loving to each other, holding and touching each other, etc.*

## Scene 2. Life in the Garden

GOD: Of every tree of the garden you may freely eat, but of the Tree of Knowledge of Good and Evil you shall not; for in the day that you eat thereof, you shall die. Now, keep faith with each other, be fruitful, multiply, and replenish the earth, and have joy.

*(Exit God and Jehovah. Enter Satan, sly but congenial, the deadly deceiver, the master manipulator.)*

SATAN: Adam, you must eat the fruit of this tree. It will make you wise.

ADAM: Are wisdom and knowledge plucked of the same tree?

SATAN: Perhaps not, but knowledge is the beginning of wisdom.

ADAM: Regardless, I must not partake of it.

SATAN: I see. *(To Eve)* Eve, this is the fruit of the Tree of

Knowledge of Good and Evil. To partake is be entrusted with knowledge.

EVE: But Father said that in the day we ate thereof we would surely die.

SATAN: Think not of death, but of knowledge!

EVE: But must knowledge come only by sorrow?

SATAN: In much wisdom is much grief; and he that increases knowledge increases sorrow *(see Eccles 1:18).*

EVE *(fearful):* But I so fear the price: *eternal sorrow.*

SATAN: Knowledge excels ignorance as joy excels sorrow.

EVE (shrinking back): But I so fear the price: *eternal darkness.*

SATAN: Knowledge dispels darkness.

EVE, trembling: But I so fear the price: even *eternal death!*

SATAN: Think not of death. To have knowledge is to be like God!

EVE (reflective): God, who comprehends all, is all good. I will partake.

*(Eve eats.)*

SATAN: Now go and plant the seed of the fruit in Adam's heart.

*(Exit Satan. Eve, trembling with trepidation, approaches Adam.)*

EVE: Adam, I have eaten the fruit of the Tree of Knowledge of Good and Evil.

ADAM *(devastated):* Eve! The snug garden of our life is to be consumed by a hot summer sun--a sun which will set in sadness, my heart says, to rise no more.

EVE (*in contemplative awe, hand on heart:)* In *my* heart are strange contradictions. It is all so new to me! On the right I feel guilt, and yet, on the left, justification. At the base of my heart is sadness: I have not kept faith with you, and I have disobeyed God by partaking of the fruit of the tree. And yet above all, I feel hope. I see the promise of

knowledge. But in the center of my heart I know I must leave the Garden, and you will be left naive and unfeeling, alone. Darling Adam, what shall we do? *(They embrace.)*

ADAM: Am I so quickly separated from love? Is my destiny to be the Garden of Nothingness? Between fear and nothing, I must choose fear. Between death and nothing, I must choose death.

*(Adam eats.)*

EVE: Yes, in partaking, I too fear death; but more, I fear never knowing life in its fullness.

ADAM: No, death is not the greatest fear. I fear most what must die with us--all that we learn, all that we come to know will be no more. The fruits of the tree will perish with us. How very strange!

EVE *(reflective):* But when we planted the fruits of the Tree, I perceive we also sowed seeds of hope.

ADAM: Yes, and I begin to perceive we are yet naked in knowledge, yet unclad in wisdom, and must yet adorn ourselves with the garments of consciousness.

EVE: And we are not yet like gods.

*(Reenter God and Jehovah.)*

GOD: Adam and Eve, you both have eaten of the Tree of the Knowledge of Good and Evil. Because you have disobeyed, you must journey *alone* upon the face of the land, to die in sorrow on a distant shore. For dust thou art and unto dust shalt thou return (see *Gen 2*).

ADAM: But are we eternally lost? Must we wander through life in total solitude? In death, is this dust to be forever blown before the wind?

JEHOVAH *(with compassion):* Neither death, nor life, nor angels, nor powers, nor things present, nor things to come, shall be able to separate us from the love of our Father (see *Romans 8:38*).

EVE *(ecstatic):* Oh, death, where then is thy sting? Oh, grave, where then is thy victory? (see *1 Cor. 15:55*).

ADAM *(ecstatic):* If this be true, then let us die the death of the righteous! (see *Num 23:10*).

*(They embrace.)*

GOD: Adam and Eve, you must leave our presence, but I will bestow upon you the priesthood, that you may act in our names, and I will provide messengers who will come bearing light and knowledge. My son, see that Adam and Eve are borne into the lone and dreary world, where they may learn by their own experiences the conflicts of ignorance and the loneliness of knowledge, and where they may develop faith.

**Scene 3. IN THE WORLD**

*(Lights up upon Adam, Eve, and their son Seth in the world, many years later; two adult children (men or women) are nearby, stage left, working at hand crafts, e.g, shoe repair, sewing; Adam, Eve, and Seth are standing over an alter, arms raised in supplication. Enter Satan, stage right, dressed as a man.)*

SATAN: I saw you praying. What is it you want?

ADAM: Knowledge. But *who* are you?

SATAN: I am Satan. I am a Son of God. What is it you want?

ADAM: God promised to send messengers to us with light and knowledge. But from *where* did you come?

SATAN: I am always close about. If you look, you will find me. What is it you want?

ADAM: Greater understanding. But *why* have you come?

SATAN: To teach you the truth about God. Can you believe in a God who is without passions, who sits on a majestic throne of impartiality, who ignores the comings and going of humankind, and who fills the universe and yet cannot touch your heart?

ADAM: No. I cannot comprehend such a God.

SATAN: Perhaps you can more easily understand hell, that great fiery pit, full of guilt and unforgiving, into which are cast the doubting and meddlesome, where they may burn eternally.

ADAM: No, it is difficult to believe in such a place.

SATAN *(shrugs his shoulders in frustration and, as an aside, explains to SETH):* Some people *only* believe in that which is difficult to believe.

SETH: Some beliefs are more dangerous than lies.

SATAN *(To Adam):* Well, if you cannot believe, then accept what I say by faith.

ADAM: We are not required to trust in that which is not of God.

EVE: True faith comes not of a man, but of God.

*(Freeze during first and second children's discussion stage left, out of ear-shot of Adam and Eve.)*

FIRST CHILD: Father prefers discernment over blind belief. He doubts the teachings of Satan.

SECOND CHILD: So it seems. But Father has never lacked faith since leaving the Garden. Are faith and belief not identical?

FIRST CHILD: No. Faith is a bridge that gaps the chasm separating the unknown from the known. Belief is a trail that winds down and across the chasm, but the trail may not always reach the heights.

SECOND CHILD: Thank God for the bridge. But what then of belief's opposite, doubt? Is doubt not also the opposite of faith?

FIRST CHILD: Be sure, my brother (or sister): Doubt need not be unfaithfulness. Indeed, uncertainties are the headwaters of the chasm. Without them faith would be unnecessary.

SECOND CHILD: Faith fits nicely among God's four other gifts: love, forgiveness, knowledge, and time.

(Center stage.)

SETH *(to ADAM):* Father, what do you think of this man's teachings?

ADAM: Since I cannot comprehend him, I cannot believe what he teaches.

SETH: Yes, there are perils in the unknown, but false beliefs are even more perilous.

ADAM *(wearily):* Even so, there remains much that is unknown to us.

EVE *(reflective):* When we were yet in the Garden, God promised to send light and knowledge through messengers.

SATAN: I am such a messenger . . . and I can work miracles to prove it.

*(Freeze during dialogue of first and second children stage left, again.)*

FIRST CHILD: This man misrepresents the power of God's messengers; messengers only endow light and knowledge.

SECOND CHILD: Is that not enough?

FIRST CHILD: Father and Mother will be happy enough.

SECOND CHILD: Miracles mean little for those who are happy.

*(Center Stage again.)*

SETH: I perceive that God has already sent many messengers. *(Points to Adam and Eve)* You are messengers for each other. Even this man *(points to Satan)* could be a messenger if he spoke truth. The stars, the land, the oceans, the rivers and streams, trees, animals and fishes of all variety--all of God's creations--these are His messengers. But we must search for their light and knowledge, and store away their messages in our consciousness.

SATAN: But then you cannot have all light and all knowledge until some gray and misty day in the dim future.

ADAM: *(Disappointed)* And then only by the sweat of our brows.

EVE: Yes, but we had our eyes opened in the garden; and if these messengers linger, faith becomes the messenger, perhaps the greatest of them all.

ADAM: *(Understanding)* Faith will sustain us until that day.

EVE: *(With joy)* And then we shall be like God.

*(Adam and Eve embrace.)*

## Chapter 7

## All The News Fit To Print

*Note: Some critics of the Church seem to assume that negative and conflicting information on the origins of the Church would destroy the faith of members. The following newspaper stories suggest another possibility. Incidentally, this story was written in 1982, at least two years before the public controversy over the "White Salamander Letter" and other recent historic finds.*

***New York Post* —Monday, November 1**

**MORMON CHURCH ANNOUNCES FIND**
***Letter Rumored to Cast Doubt on Founder***

(UPI—Salt Lake City) B. Glen Jones, a spokesman for the Salt Lake-based Church of Jesus Christ of Latter-day Saints (Mormon), today announced acquisition of a letter written by Joseph Smith, church founder. The letter, which was not made public, is rumored to throw doubt on the claimed divine origin of the Book of Mormon.

The letter, written to Seth Stowell of Pennsylvania, is dated January 16, 1830, the year of the church's organization. Stowell, son of a former Smith employer, was a friend of Smith's during the years he lived in upstate New York.

The letter was discovered in a waxed-tin box in the home of Mrs. Lucy Jacobs, great grand-daughter of Stowell. She contacted an antiques dealer in Philadelphia, who put her in touch with Herbert V. Mathews, University of Utah Historical Museum Director, and a private collector of historical Mormon documents. Mathews eventually bought the letter for a yet-unnamed price.

"When I first saw the document, I thought it was probably authentic and valuable," Mathews told the press. Mathews had the letter authenticated in New York City before re-selling it to an unnamed person who recently donated the letter to the Mormon Church. The document has been declared a "monumental find" by Dr. Lynn Tanner, a BYU history professor and an authority on the life of Joseph Smith.

The Church's announcement said the text of the letter was being carefully studied by scholars of the church. "No one should jump to any conclusions," it stressed. No summary of the contents was included. Gary and Sharril Romney, vocal anti-Mormons living in Salt Lake, claimed to have seen a copy. The letter was "proof that Smith was a fraud," he said. He declined further comment until the letter was released. "It's really going to hit the fan," he told a UPI reporter by phone.

*New York Post* **--Thursday, November 4**

**MORMON CHURCH RELEASES TEXT OF LETTER**
*Founder's Motives Questioned by Detractors*

(UPI--Salt Lake City) The Church of Jesus Christ of Latter-day Saints (Mormon) today released the text of a mysterious letter thought to be written in August 1830 by Joseph Smith, founder of the Salt Lake-based church. The letter is addressed to Seth Stowell, a friend of Smith's during his youth. An accompanying one-page press release cautioned Mormon Church members against over reacting and promised further information.

In the letter, Smith claims to have written the Book of Mormon with the help of family and friends for "a worthy perpose. I wrote it under inspiration to clarify the disparat teachings of the holy Bible which foolish ministers were preaching in this county. The book sold quite well, and I fell into the habit of letting others make egsaggerated claims about the book which seemed to titilate the local gentry. I thought it harmless, and was gratified by the serius recepsion the book got from folks." Smith also wrote, "Gradually, a number of fine people have come to view me as their leader, and I am become their leader through the grace of God."

In the letter Smith asks Stowell for advice on leading his followers. According to Dr. Lynn Tanner, a noted historian at BYU, "Joseph Smith appears involved in circumstances that even he didn't seem to fully understand. As you know, he became the leader of a faithful Christian people."

It is not clear from the letter whether Smith believed in the divine origins of the book himself. "That which is wrought of God is eternal trueth," he wrote in the letter's last paragraph. The letter does not say why Smith wrote to Stowell in particular, but Gary Romney, a local Mormon Church critic told the press that Smith was probably feeling guilty and needed to tell someone he trusted. "We've been expecting a smoking pistol like this for a long time," he told a UPI reporter.

The LDS Church news release said scholars were studying the text. It urged Mormons not to pre-judge the motives of the "prophet," and suggested that Smith may have been under duress when he wrote the letter. Even the Apostle Peter made questionable statements under pressure, the news release said.

***New York Post* — Saturday, November 6**

## LDS CHURCH EXPLAINS LETTER
***Mormons Numbed***

(UPI—Salt Lake City) The First Presidency of the Church of Jesus Christ of Latter-day Saints (Mormon) today told church faithful that Joseph Smith, the church's founder, wrote a letter in 1830 which "could be interpreted to cast doubt on the authenticity of the Book of Mormon," a book Smith also claimed was given him by an angel. In an announcement released to members yesterday, the First Presidency stressed that Smith's motives, thoughts, and feelings at the time are unknown. The article said the letter could be a blow to Smith's credibility, if taken literally and out of context.

Gary Romney, a vocal anti-Mormon, claims the Mormon church is in deep trouble. "Joseph Smith was a false prophet and the Church is practically admitting it. How can members continue to support the church?" he challenged in a letter-to-the-editor of a Salt Lake newspaper this morning.

Asked about the 1830 Smith letter, Mormons on Salt Lake's Main Street were mostly unresponsive to a UPI reporter's questions. "I don't know what to think," was a common reply. Most said they had not yet seen the letter and were waiting for the First Presidency's explanation.

B. Glen Jones, official church spokesman, asked yesterday why the letter was released, said, "We rarely keep anything from our members. We teach correct principles and allow members to govern themselves." He went on to say that truth was paramount, no matter what effect it might have. "We can stand an open light on any document," he said.

**New York Post —Monday, November 8**

**MORMONS RESPOND TO LETTER**
***Attendance and Offerings Unaffected***

(UPI—Salt Lake City) Yesterday's attendance at LDS church meetings was reported to be higher than normal. A telephone poll of ten bishops of local congregations in the Salt Lake City area brought reports of business as usual. "At our monthly Testimony Meetings a lot of members reaffirmed their commitment to the Church," several bishops reported. Offerings were said to be about normal.

When asked why members would continue to support the Church in spite of recent developments, B. Glen Jones, official church spokesman said, "Most members have received independant witnesses to the truthfulness of the Church and Christ's teachings. Whatever else happens, the Church is Christ's church."

Gary Romney, vocal critic of the Mormon Church, asserted that the Church was so entwined in the everyday life of members that a sudden explosion was unlikely. "When your whole life has been engulfed by one single precept, when your entire social and business life is tied closely to one central authority, things can't change quickly," he said. He was surprised, however, by the lack of defections. "I'd have expected to see a few more, really."

Dr. Lynn Tanner, a BYU historian and an expert on Joseph Smith, told UPI that a few intellectuals in the church had already discounted some of the claims made for Joseph Smith. "Another letter isn't going to make much difference," he said. "This only makes it easier for some to be more objective about Joseph Smith, and to see him as human."

**New York Post—Monday, December 24**

## LDS CHURCH LEADERS EXPRESS OPTIMISM
***Members Keep the Faith***

(UPI—Salt Lake City) Leaders of the Church of Jesus Christ of Latter-day Saints (Mormon) today expressed optimism for a continued bright future. In a Christmas message, the First Presidency thanked members for their continued support. "Given the events of the past two months, it is gratifying to witness the continued faithfulness of our members," they said. "It shows the true love of Christ in each of you. We have great missions to accomplish on this earth, and we have the will and means to accomplish them."

George C. Smith, First Counselor in the church's First Presidency, expressed optimism in a news interview with UPI reporters. "In a sense, the burden of certainty has been lifted from our shoulders," Smith said. "The emphasis has shifted slightly. It isn't as important to gain a testimony of the Joseph Smith story as in the past. Rather the emphasis has shifted to developing a testimony of Christ and to following His teachings."

Gary Romney, outspoken critic of the Church, is "dismayed" at the response of Mormons to recent events. "Either they're totally brain-washed, or I've been mistaken. I can't understand how the Mormon Church keeps bouncing back from disaster," he told reporters last week.

President Smith responded to this statement by saying, "Because the Mormon Church teaches true Christian principles, and because it is a beacon of hope and love on a dark horizon, it is ordained to be strong and healthy, in spite of its imperfectly understood origins."

# Chapter 8

## The Evidence of Things Not Seen

*Faith is the evidence of things not seen.* -- (Heb. 11:1)

*In the 1990's, almost anyone can have access to the contents of entire libraries at the touch of a button, right at home. This accessibility raises questions and concerns about the use and misuse of information which has hitherto been protected by its unavailability.*

*For example, the Church's historical repositories presumably contain many sacred or potentially controversial documents which have been restricted to legitimate researchers. The potential for universal access of this information (and potential misuse of it) presents two options. First, the Church could live with the problem, trusting that a knowledgeable membership will draw positive conclusions and that those inoculated by germs of criticisms will be made resistant to apostasy. Or conversely, additional restrictions on access could be made, thereby preventing contact with the information altogether.*

*This is the story of the second option, and its effect on one individual.*

It was Heber's letter to the morning paper that really caused some trouble.

Until that day Heber Tanner had been a faithful Mormon. Clean-cut, as solid as the temple foundation, and fresh out of BYU with an MA in history, he had been retained as a junior assistant researcher at the Church's Historical Department—quite a showing of trust. Very few people had been allowed into the department, much less work there, since the strict access restrictions imposed ten years before.

In those days, Heber was a precocious senior at Salt Lake's East High School. Shunning sports and the like, but excited by religion, social issues, and history, he had paid close attention to the arguments which flashed between ecclesiastical leaders and Mormon intellectuals, as reported in the newspapers. Of course, he had sided with the Church. No sense giving enemies of the church a chance to distort the truth, he had concluded. Heber's father, a bishop at the time, had solidly backed the Church's new policy. Honest men, he told Heber, men called of God, would still have access to the records. It wasn't as if the records were sealed up completely. The Church would provide any necessary information. Heber was a true believer, in both his father and the Church. It all made good sense. And sealing up religious records was not all that rare. Joseph Smith was given records which were partially sealed.

"It fits God's purposes to withhold some types of information," he had told his ward at his missionary farewell. During his mission in Texas, Heber became a staunch proselytizer and fervent testimony-bearer. He felt the Lord's spirit regularly. On one occasion, the spirit directed him and his companion to the door of one eventual convert; on another, Heber healed a sister suffering from asthma. He had had only one questionable experience. A golden couple—loving, kind, full of the Spirit—Brother and Sister Ortega, called at the last minute to decline baptism. They mentioned having had an eye-opening experience that changed their minds about the Church. Heber responded like a sleepwalker awakened suddenly in a thunderstorm. Emotions flashed crazily through his mind like bolts of lightning: surprise ("My God, how could this have happened?"), fear ("Whose fault is this—mine?"), frustration ("Why do my investigators keep quitting?"), desperation and anquish ("Will this never end?"), guilt ("Did I push too hard? Too fast? Am I living righteously?"), betrayal ("Why has the Lord foresaken me?"), anger ("What did I do to deserve this? Why does the damned devil interfer?"), doubt ("What does this all mean? Is God really involved?"), concern ("What will the other elders think? What will happen to the souls of my investigators?"), and disappointment ("They were so golden!")

Heber fasted and prayed for two days, but to no avail. The Ortegas were not only not ready, they rejected any further contact with him or the Church. He settled into a sullen, dull depression. Heber's mission president eventually transferred him to another area, hoping to pull him out of the hole. That seemed to help. A week later, Heber's letter was again tinted with the pinks and golds of hope and promise. The Ortega's failure was seen as test, a strengthening experience purposely provided by a loving Father. Stability, purpose, and confidence returned to Heber's mind.

His mission completed, he departed for BYU, married Joan, fathered two children in successive years, and finished two degrees. The new job at the Historical Department was the next step in what seemed a foreordained destiny to be one of the chosen, one of the champions of the faith.

During the first few months, Heber had the task of compiling historical information for General Authorities who were writing books or preparing talks and speeches. Heber received no publication credit, but he knew that he had to serve a worthy stewardship before he could hope to become a recognized Church historian or author. Heber was content to play the role of a patient missionary waiting for the Spirit—one cannot push too fast or too hard when it came to Church matters.

After three months on the job, Brother Stevenson, one of the assistant historians, asked Heber to come in to discuss a new assignment. Brother Stevenson was in his early fifties, a former bishop, and a forty-acre farmer of history. Slightly graying in his thinning side-burns, soft-spoken and wise, a twenty-year veteran of the department, he had quickly become Heber's model. "You'll have access to Early Records Room No. 3," he said solemnly. "You know the worth of original documents. Limit your handling of them. Use the microfilm when possible. Always sign in and out at the desk. And always wear these gloves when you handle any actual documents." He handed Heber a pair of clear PVC plastic gloves.

"As you know, Room No 3. contains materials associated with Parley P. Pratt, Heber C. Kimball, and most of Brigham Young's wives. And I believe we still have some early materials from the Smith family library stored in there." Brother Stevenson stood up, smiling slightly. His clothes hung loose on his wiry body. He looked more like a clerk than an historian. He gave Heber a friendly pat on the back and the standard Department admoniton, "Keep your eyes on your work."

Heber's new task was to review and summarize materials associated with Brigham Young's family life, as recorded in Brigham's wives' journals. Albert O. Young, a member of the First Quorum of Seventy, and a descendant of Brigham Young was writing a book about early Mormon family life.

Discussing the assignment with Brother Stevenson at lunch a week later, Heber observed carefully that this might be the opportunity he had been waiting for. Maybe Brother Young would recognize his help in the book's Foreword, maybe even in the book's dedicatory paragraph?

"Aren't you pushing just a bit?" Brother Stevenson asked gently. "It might help to remember the admonition to have 'an eye single to the glory' of the Lord."

"Mmmm," Heber blushed. No pushing, he remembered.

That evening, walking home in the winter fog to his little apartment on Second Avenue, Heber wondered what the Lord had in mind for him. What could his purpose be in placing him in the department? Surely not just to be somebody's researcher. In almost every other library in the country, the work he was doing would be done in seconds by computers. What did it all mean? He shivered and hurried on through the icy fog.

Each day for several weeks, Heber obtained the key and quietly let himself into the small room. It felt like a vault—clean, mysterious, and solid. A heavy table stood in the center, a microfilm reader on one end. Old library-style green shelving lined the walls on three sides. Assorted metal-trimmed wooden boxes contained the ancient documents. An inlet air register at one corner hissed quietly with air, controlled for temperature and humidity.

The room always seemed cool and moist so Heber wore his suit coat. He felt more respectful anyway. As the days passed, Heber mentally catalogued the major containers in the room. All were extremely interesting. But Heber kept to his stewardship—the microfilm labeled, "Brigham Young Wives."

Storage boxes were identified by yellowing labels, typed years ago with a hand typewriter. "B. H. Roberts's work?" Heber wondered with awe. A small, sturdy wood and metal box contained materials labeled, "Family Library #4, J. Smith, Sr., New York." Heber was tempted to look in, but he knew he'd feel guilty if he did.

One Friday afternoon, Heber entered the room and flipped on the light. As the door closed, he noticed that the "Library #4" box was open. Someone must have been in the room during lunch and had forgotten to close the box. After a bit of internal debate, Heber's curiosity forced him, against his own instincts, to the box. He cautiously lifted several documents from the darkness. His gloved hands trembled as he contemplated the Prophet himself holding those very same papers.

Disappointment came quickly. The box contained only old newspapers, periodicals, pamphlets, and protestant religious tracts. Somehow Heber had expected to see handwritten letters, notes, diaries. Now he realized that such items would be in the First Presidency's Vault.

Heber carefully carried to the center table a yellowing and brittle copy of an old newspaper, Wayne Sentinel, folded open to page 3. Standing over the document, squinting, Heber was barely able to read the blurred and irregular type. A small article in the lower corner had been underscored by someone years ago. It was entitled, "Infant Baptism—A Corruption." The article appeared to be a strong condemnation of the practice of infant baptism.

He looked at the author and date at the bottom of the article—"Dec. 2, 1829, A. Campbell, N.Y." Somewhere it seemed to Heber that he had read this same material, and recently, too. "Yes...but when?" he asked aloud.

Then it struck him. He sat down heavily, chilled. Heb opened his briefcase and brought out his missionary scriptures, thumbing quickly to Moroni. He carefully compared the article to Chapter 8, verses 5 through 22.

They were very similar—in some passages identical! Heber looked again at the date of the article.

"Dec. 2, 1829."

He carefully opened the paper to the front page. Yes, the date must have been correct. The newspaper was dated, "December 20, 1829."

Heber sat for several minutes not moving. His eyes glazed as he stared at the paper. Here was a newspaper article, very similar to passages from the Book of Mormon, written the year before the publication of the Book of Mormon, in a newspaper kept in the home of the Smith family. It was a library to which Joseph Smith had access. Heber suddenly remembered the Ortegas' eye-opening experience and thought he understood. He lifted his newly opened eyes to the ceiling. "Joseph Smith must have copied Moroni 8 from the Wayne Sentinel," he whispered, his voice fading and high. Goose bumps cascaded down his chest and arms. He stood and leaned against the wall, his six-foot frame bent slightly at the waist. His knees weakened and he moved to sit again. The room seemed to darken; the walls moved in towards him. He felt nauseous and fought off the urge to throw up. His vision blurred. He lowered his head onto the table and cried.

Except for the experience with the Ortegas, Heber had always been able to avoid questions and doubts. Suddenly it was clear to him that everything in his life had been a shield, a wall to reduce the influences of the world and of Satan. He was the offspring of a system designed to protect, not to strengthen, a system intended to isolate, not to immunize.

Never in his life had Heber felt so assaulted, so invaded. In the space of a few moments a smooth and gentle plain of belief and belonging had been wrenched into a jagged chasm of doubt and alienation—from the Church, from Joseph, even from God. Heber sat, quietly regaining a measure of composure. Anger and betrayal swept through him. He wanted revenge. He stood, flipped off the light, went to his office, and quickly composed two letters—one to the morning paper describing his discovery and his sudden need to help others see the truth about the Book of Mormon. The other was a letter of immediate resignation addressed to Brother Stevenson. On his way out he dropped both letters in the mail slot. The resignation would probably hit Brother Stevenson's desk Monday morning.

Friday night was hell. Fortunately, his wife and children were in Arizona visiting her parents. Picking at the pieces, thinking this and that, Heber spent the night alone, pacing the little apartment. He didn't feel like calling friends or family yet—what would they say? His news would devastate them, too. He wasn't ready for that. It took a couple of aspirins to get to sleep.

Sometime after three, he awoke to the smell of smoke. Struggling up, he looked out the window to see a smoldering garbage can below. The lights of the city had dimmed, but he could hear a siren way off in the distance. Stumbling down the stairs, he searched in vain for the lid to extinquish the fire. Suddenly they were there, dousing the fire with extinquishers: just as suddenly, they were gone—two firemen dressed for a much bigger fire. Climbing back to his room, he sat for a long time looking out the window. He could see nothing of the fire, but he could smell lingering smoke.

On Saturday and Sunday, his mood dulled, and he even had a few fleeting moments without pain. He tried to plan the next few weeks, and to think about the future, but his emotions kept getting in the way. Several thoughts kept coming back, "How could they have done this to us? Damn! How!? Why would God do this to me? Why?"

The letter to the morning paper, the one that eventually caused so much trouble, appeared in the paper Monday morning. About nine-thirty, Heber received a call from from Brother Stevenson.

"Heber, I just opened my mail and your letter. And I've just been handed a copy of the morning paper. I'm shocked. I don't know what to say. Could you come down and tell me about all this?"

Heber said yes, he'd be down shortly. Heber wondered how Brother Stevenson was handling the faith-killing information. Would Brother Stevenson quit the Church, too? Heber felt bad about being the messenger bearing sad tidings, but what else could he have done?

At the office, Heber recounted his experience quickly as Brother Stevenson listened without moving, worry and concern visible as he listened.

When Heber finished, Brother Stevenson stood and walked around the desk. "Heber, why didn't you ask me? Don't you think we know about this thing already? We believe that Joseph wrote the article and submitted it to Wayne Sentinel under a pen name. He must have translated that section and wanted to float a trial balloon prior to the printing of the Book of Mormon." He put his arms around Heber.

Heber sat unspeaking, his eyes tightly shut.

"Of course, we don't know for certain what happened," Brother Stevenson said gently. "No evidence, however devastating, can survive against faith. Nothing we can see can ever be as valuable as that which we cannot see."

# Chapter 9

## Believing for Dollars

*I respect faith, but doubt is what gets you an education.* -- Wilson Mizner

*Much has been said about some Mormons having unreasonable faith in get-rich-quick schemes being sponsored by "trustworthy" Mormons.*

*Having faith in fellow Mormons and what they say and do is an important facet of our religion. Many of us have our faith strengthened by hearing others bear their testimonies, and we certainly are expected to have faith in decisions made by our leaders. Therefore, it is not surprising that some make the jump from spiritual to temporal to economic faith, especially when such things have their origin in the same mouth, and sometimes in the same breath.*

*This is the story of an Olympic-class broad jumper.*

"Buy low, sell high." That's the first commandment for stock brokers, real estate people, and other smart folks like my Sunday School teacher, Brother Jones. Me? I've always bought high and sold low. That is until last September when Brother Jones invited me to a seminar, "How to Buy and Sell Off-Season for Fun and Profit." It's pretty simple—you find something off-season cheap, then sell it at a higher price during the regular season. The secret is believing. You've got to believe in yourself and the program. And you've got to have a good contact.

Anyway, about a week later, Brother Jones called about an off-season deal, and I made my first buy. It was pretty simple. Brother Jones, you see, is a salesman and his discount company was clearing out somebody's over-stocked motorcycles. I had him save one for me. I couldn't believe it—a new motorcycle at the ridiculously low price of $1,000. And a beauty it was—sleek, black, and cheap.

Brother Jones is kind of a big, outgoing guy—always talking and laughing. He's the kind of guy you can trust. He knows something about almost everything. And he's always given me good advice. This time was no exception. I remember he slapped the contoured seat with his hand and said, "Drive it all fall and sell it in the spring for a handsome profit."

And that's just what I did, sort of. Unfortunately, winter arrived a bit early last year—about October 1st. I didn't get in a lot of riding.

"Oh, well," I later explained to my wife Cindi, "a low-mileage bike will sell even faster in the spring."

"Right," she said. "Twenty-seven miles should be real attractive to somebody."

"Very funny,", I said. "When I make a killing on this deal, you'll see." Cindi's not much into risk taking. She sticks to her needle work and the kids mostly.

Spring arrived this year a wee behind schedule. People were still skiing Snowbird on June 25th. And there was an abnormal amount of rain and cool weather in the valley. But these tiny impediments didn't cool my enthusiasm for getting on with the killing. (It was too cold to ride the machine, anyway.)

In June, I put a cheap 2-liner in the want-ads.

> Almost new Cycle. exec cond. low price.
> low miles. See to appreciate.

Not one call! But it was a learning experience. In the next ad, I remembered to put in my telephone number.

The second ad got a couple of calls. On the first one, we were inexplicably disconnected right after I quoted $1050. (By now, my conscience had gotten the best of me. I didn't really want to take advantage of anyone. I'd get my money out and call it my training experience. Nothing like a little success to spur one on.) The next call was from the woman next door. "If that lame-brained son of mine calls, tell him I absolutely refuse to have one of those death traps around," she almost shouted.

"Look, Mrs. Nelson, they're not death traps...and I'll throw in a helmet..." She hung up. Her son never called. No one did. It was time to get aggressive.

I opened the newspaper to the want-ads under "Motorcycles." At first I thought I must have been in the "Houses for Sale" section. Column after column after column. Hondas by the herd loads. Suzuki, Yamaha, Kawasaki—it looked like a Japanese invasion of the mainland. The lowest price for a bike like mine—$900. "What a piece of junk that must be," I said aloud, shaking my head.

"You talking about the motorcycle?" Cindi asked, not looking up from her cross stitch.

"Hardy, har, har! Funny lady...I better call this guy and see what's the matter with his bike," I said, dialing.

He wasn't home but his wife said he had eighty-four miles on the machine. Seems he knew this salesman down at this discount store....

I told her thanks. She asked if I had sold my bike. "How do you know I've got one for sale?" I asked.

"You're the third guy that's called with the same kind of bike for sale."

I didn't like her tone, so I politely slammed the receiver down. My next call was to Brother Jones. "Last fall, you said..."

I heard his pudgy hand slap the seat of a motorcycle nearby. "Who'd ever thought the weather would turn so sour, brother! You think you got troubles! Come on down here! We've got another fifty of that same model selling, so to speak, at $995."

Fortunately, he came through for me again, giving me some good advice on selling the bike. My next want-ad looked professional:

*** LOOK! SPECIAL! LOOK! ***
Almost New Cycle. Must sell this weekend. Low miles. Rack. Lots of extras. Windshield, brand new. Skirts. Extra low miles. Unheard of low price. Only $999!! See to appreciate,—etc

The ad cost $27 to run for the weekend, but I was desperate. The silly bike was threatening our budget. (Brother Jones said lots of extras hanging on the bike would sell it fast. So I bought about $200 of bike accessories out of July's rent.)

This time, it worked. I got almost eleven calls! (One hung up before I got to the phone.) Five of the calls were to see if I wanted to trade up. I didn't. Four were checking to see if I had gotten lucky. I hadn't. One was from the next-door neighbor again. I promised I wouldn't sell to her son.

When August rolled around, I sat and gave the problem a long, thoughtful evaluation—just like we do down at the office. The solution finally hit me—direct sales! I went and bought one of those black and red *FOR SALE* signs, a steel chain, and a big stainless steel lock. Wheeling over to the corner of 39th South and 13th East, I chained it to the traffic signal post, went home, and waited for the calls to start coming.

I imagined crowds of people standing around admiring the sleek black body, all waxed, low miles, and all. The price? A ridiculous $895! I saw young men racing each other for the nearest phone. And my wait was not long. A polite but gruff voice came on the other end of the phone.

"You gotta bike tied down over here on da corner?" he mumbled. I wondered if he had any money.

"Yeah, you interested? I can be flexible on the price."

"Nope. My wife says we're getting kitchen carpet first. Anyway, we just impounded it. Section 40-32a of the county code. Can't tie down to our pole, ya know that?"

"No I didn't know that," I said innocently.

"You can get it down at the county yard, next Tuesday. Ya gotta go in ta see Judge Butcher, first, though."

"Gee, ah, I'm awfully sorry. Maybe if I just ran right over?" (No way.) "Well, what about the cost?"

"Yes, sir. Ahhh, $45 for towing, $11 for storage, that's per day; $26 court costs, plus whatever Judge Butcher says you gotta pay in fines."

Sounds disastrous, doesn't it? Well, I guess you have to have faith that things will work out—during the trip to the county yard, the bike fell off the truck and was totalled. All county costs were forgiven. The insurance company paid "fair market value."

"Just what was fair market value?" Cindi asked in a cute tone of voice like she didn't really care.

"Never mind," I said. "Just keep to your knitting and leave the wheeling and dealing to me. It was fair. That's all we could hope for, right? We couldn't predict the weather, right?"

"Right," she said, biting through a stray bit of thread. "By the way, Brother Jones called about some unsold, distressed electronic barbeques. He said he has some real good off-season prices. He'll let you to buy a couple for quick resale this coming summer."

"Wow! Where's the ward roster?"

"I think I lost it," she said in her please-don't-ever-do-it-again voice.

I can take a hint. No more wheeling and dealing. It was fun, though, just like they said at the seminar.

# Chapter 10

# The Knowledge Machine

*Humans are curious. We prefer knowledge over uncertainty. We like to ask questions, particularly if they can be answered, and especially if they can be answered quickly and accurately.*

*The more information we can collect to answer our questions the better we like it. We often go to expensive extremes to improve the response time, accuracy, and reliability of information sources: we built x-ray machines, then the CAT Scanner. The electron microscope followed the light microscope, and the slide rule preceded the calculator and computer.*

*Microelectronics is opening vast new frontiers in almost all fields of knowledge development. Pocket-sized memory devices can store millions of bits of information. Central Processing Units (CPUs) are able to analyze thousands of inputs in seconds. Wave energy receivers are becoming so sensitive that radio wave energy created at the dawn of the universe is being measured and recorded.*

*Scientists have long suspected that people are capable of nonsensory communication, e.g., mental telepathy. Some theorize that such communications may come through actual human transmission of radio frequencies heretofore unmeasurable, and that a person actually radiates, or broadcasts, whatever thoughts and feelings are in his or her mind. Some have said that God Himself uses such radiations to communicate information.*

*This is the story of a man with a desperate need to reduce uncertainty and find quick, accurate answers.*

"Bishop Sanders

The soft voice on the phone sounded familiar. "Yes . . . Sister Smith? You sound upset. Can I do something for you?"

"Oh. . . aah. . . look, I just need to talk to you. Something awful has happened. . . with my fiance. I need to talk." Her voice cracked.

"Okay. But let's not talk over the phone. Why don't you meet me at my office at the church in, ahh, 33 minutes--seven-thirty p.m., okay?"

Bishop Sanders slowly placed the phone in it's cradle, sighed, and walked into the kitchen. "I'm sorry, Sal, but I've got to get over to the ward by seven-thirty. One of the sisters just called and needs to talk to me."

Sally Sanders put down the dish towel. "Being bishop is hard on you, isn't it?" she said.

The bishop sighed again. "I have to learn to live with it. I've just got to reprogram myself, that's all."

Sally came and softly put her arms around his neck. She hung lightly, like a feather resting on the edge of a high shelf.

"You've been a big help so far, Sal. I appreciate it," he said methodically. Sally looked small against the tall man. Thin and graying, he looked older than his wife, although they both were thirty-nine. "I'd better get over there." His chronograph showed less than twenty-three minutes to the appointment.

In his office, Bishop Sanders waited behind his desk. The new fluorescent lights overhead revealed his reflection in the polished desk surface. He was startled to see how somber he looked. Three months as bishop was taking its toll.

An electrical engineer by training, he found people's personal problems baffling and maddeningly complicated--not at all like the straight forward engineering equations he dealt with at work. Things follow laws, he thought. Put 110 volts through a 55 ohm resistor and you always get 2 amps. Simple. Consistent. Easy to learn. Easy to understand. Why can't people follow laws? he wondered.

Reaching for his briefcase, he pulled out a small metal box covered with dials, meters, lights, and a digital tuner. A floppy six-inch antenna.

arose from the top. This might help, he thought hopefully. His company was building this instrument for the government, and he had one of the few prototypes built for testing. A marvel of sensitivity, it could identify, evaluate, and store the subtle radio frequencies emitted by humans during conversation. In some ways it was related to the old lie-detector, but this instrument could recognize sincerity and insincerity, love and hate, belief and doubt, sorrow, repentance. In short, it was just what every new bishop needed. Hearing a noise in the foyer, he replaced the box in his briefcase. Not enough time to test it now, he told himself.

Opening the office door, he squinted into the darkness of the empty foyer. Shiela Smith stood in the shadows, her head down, her hands clasped in front of her. Her eyes were red and tired-looking. She came into the office and sat stiffly in the chair across from his desk. Though obviously torn with misery, she looked pretty and was well-tanned from working in her yard.

She had bought the old Webster home several years ago and lived there alone. Independent and socially active, with a full time career, she seemed to enjoy the diversion of a little yard work. Some of the men on the street enjoyed giving her a hand. Most of the women wished she would get married. But Shiela showed no sign of getting married, even though she had a steady male friend, who worked at the university with her.

Bishop Sanders wished this were a marriage interview—happy, light, and full of excitement. "What seems to be the problem, Sister Smith?"

Tears of distress flooded Shiela's eyes. Bishop Sanders momentarily wished he could follow the formula that worked so well with his wife: take her in his arms, hold her close, put her head on his shoulder, soothe her, comfort her. But, of course, he couldn't.

"Please," he said softly, but with discomfort. "Tears won't...aah... help anything," he stumbled, hating himself for saying such a stupid thing. "Why don't you just tell me about it."

Sheila wiped her eyes with a yellow hankerchief from her leather purse, and her cheeks flushed appealingly. "I've done the worst...thing in the world. I haven't had a moment's peace this past month. I've committed an unpardonable sin. What am I going to do?"

Bishop Sanders started up. "Unpardonable sin? What do you mean?" He pulled on the collar of his white dress shirt.

"Fornication...whatever. You know, sleeping...with a man." She tugged at the wet hankerchief in her lap.

Bishop Sanders relaxed a little. He didn't know what he would have done if she had said, "Murder," or "A sin against the Holy Ghost." He knew a little about sex offenses from one previous trial. "I see. Is the man married or single? And, who is he? I think it's only fornication because you're single. It might be adultry for him if he's married. I'll have to check the handbook. Anyway. . . ." He paused, exhaled, smiled, and said, "Anyway, I don't think it's unpardonable." His voice betrayed his relief.

She brightened slightly and lifted her slender frame to a more erect position. Her blond hair curled over the neck of her brown sweater. She took a deep breath. "His name is Doug. He's married. . . but getting a divorce. He's an instructor at the university. One thing led to another and, well, we've been sleeping together for a month now. Oh, Bishop, what'll I do with this guilt?" She began to cry.

After awkwardly offering comfort, Bishop Sanders summarized the Church's procedures in this type of case. A court could be convened to examine the facts. Her repentance would be evaluated. She might be excommunicated or disfellowshipped; or perhaps no Church discipline was necessary. The outcome depended on the facts of the case and on what he knew, he explained. Sheila said she understood and asked that a date be set for a court. The bishop nodded assent.

"Who will be involved?" she asked.

"I will, of course. And my counselors, and our clerks. Is there any problem?" he asked.

"Not really, but I'd like my mom and dad to come, if that's okay."

"Fine."

"And, I guess I'm a little nervous about your counselors," she said.

The bishop blinked. "Can you tell me why?" he said.

"Well, it's probably not important, but Herc and I dated during high school; and Mike seems seems so rigid. I guess they worry me."

The Bishop thought for a moment. The procedures call for his counselors to be present, but they could be excused for cause. But how would he explain it to them? "Well, I don't think it will be a problem," he said finally.

The trial night came too quickly for the bishop. He was doubly anxious because this would be the first real test of the little blue machine. Of course, he told no one. There was a need for security, naturally; and it was there to help him alone. No one else needs to know, he reasoned. He knew he was rationalizing, but he had to make a decision about Sheila. And he had to gather as much information as possible, didn't he?

They knelt in prayer to begin. Everyone was dressed in dark and conservative Sunday-best. The white window curtains were drawn shut behind the bishop. His Counselors sat at his elbows and two clerks waited unobtrusively at one side of the room. No one looked directly at Sheila, who sat alone in the center, three feet in front of the bishop's desk. She seemed lonely, like someone sitting in the middle of an empty theater, waiting for the lights to go down. She wore a dark green suit, and her hair was pulled tight behind her head. She gripped a light green handkerchief in her lap.

Bishop Sanders began with an almost-memorized speech. "We are not here to punish. This is a court of love. We must be in tune with our Father in Heaven. The court's purpose is to fulfill the requirements for repentance. Sister Smith, please tell us in your own words what happened to bring you to this place and what you have done to repent." Cracking the desk drawer, he touched a button on the blue machine. Eight little lights began to glow. He had programmed the machine to separate, store, and eventually evaluate each of the eight voices in the room.

No one noticed him: all eyes were on Shiela, except for the clerks, who self-consciously shuffled papers and tested their pens. Sheila told her story, between long pauses and stifled tears.

Her explanation of events was factual, tactful, and really quite simple. When she finished, her mother came and placed her arm over her shoulder. Both stood and embraced. The tense feeling in the room softened.

Bishop Sanders felt the sense of peace. This might be a simple court. "I'm glad we've got that out of the way," he said. "We need to ask a few questions before we separate. And, your parents might want to say something. Let's begin with Brother Walle. Would you like to ask anything?" He glanced to his right.

Bishop Sanders could guess what was going on in the mind of Michael T. Walle, his First Counselor. Mike would be thinking that the court's purpose was to establish justice, of course. Brother Walle was letter-of-the-law strict and proud of it. He had spent many months studying the Old Testament during his mission to Alabama just five years ago. Look, don't knock it...that's one of the reasons I chose him, the Bishop told himself silently. That, and his loyalty to me, and his ability to get people to do things, he thought.

Mike Walle, his vested dark suit buttoned tightly, leaned forward and spoke slowly and carefully, his chin slightly raised, his thick hands in his lap. Mr. Control, the bishop thought. "Sister Smith, I need a few things clarified. Your partner in this...ah...sin—I understand he's a member of the Church. An elder, I believe. And I understand he was married in the temple, and now he's getting a divorce. Did your crimes...against God...occur before the divorce started? I mean, did your sleeping with him cause the marital breakup?"

Sheila looked startled. Defensively she replied, "No, no. He was getting the divorce before that."

"But didn't you encourage him to seek the divorce? Did you ever give any thought to his salvation? Did you ever consider what your enticements might do to his position in the Church?" Brother Walle leaned back, waiting.

Sheila also put her back against the chair and folded her arms. "You've got this thing all wrong. In the first place, I didn't entice him. And I didn't even know he was married, at first..."

Mike interrupted like a good television attorney, "But you soon knew and you led him on, even knowing that what you were doing was going to break up a marriage."

"I wasn't leading him on," she snapped. "He told me he was already divorced when we started going out." Her voice leveled off as she regained her composure. "Later, he told me it was 'almost final.' By the time I realized what was happening, things had gone to far. But our affair didn't break up his home."

Mike leaned forward, his hands on his knees. "This brings up another question. Sex for sex's sake is one thing. Sex as a premarital slip is another. Do you two plan to be married?"

Sheila sat straight, unspeaking. The bishop knew she hadn't anticipated these questions. He had told her that if she confessed and promised to repent, he would make the appropriate decision and she could go in peace.

"I don't know that we'll be married," she said finally. "I don't know that I really love him now. We've sort of broken up, and I don't want to think about it until everything is straightened out."

Bishop Sanders broke in, his voice easing the tension. "Thank you, Brother Walle. Perhaps we ought to move along. Do you have anything to ask, Brother Petty?"

"Yes, Bishop," he started. "Sister Smith, I know this is rough. If we can find something to make it easier on you...well, we should look for it. Maybe if could go into a little more detail ..."

Bishop Sanders looked nervously over at Herculaneum Petty. He had suggested to Herc that he might want to excuse himself because of their high school dates, but Herc had indicated that even though he had had a thing for Shiela years ago, it would not interfere now.

Herc was dressed in a blue suit slightly larger than his thin, six-foot frame. Balding early, he wore a hair piece which never sat straight. That, and his crooked glasses always made people look twice. Odd looking, but salt of the earth, they always said. Everybody's favorite cousin.

Herc continued, "Sex can be beautiful. Or, it can be animalistic...

and go against...decency. I'd like to know what you two did during your meetings. I'd like you to describe the details."

Sheila stared at Herc. "Bishop, do I have to answer this question? Does it really matter?"

Bishop Sanders felt discouraged. He had given his counselors a chance to ask questions, the normal procedure. Things weren't happening like they should—the loving spirit had disappeared. First, Mike had let his dogmatic inclinations smother his still-developing sense of love and understanding. Now, Herc was letting some base instinct govern his normally caring and innocent nature.

Bishop Sanders wanted his team to win, but he also didn't want to show any disunity. "Well now, yes...ah...Sister Smith, we're only trying to help. Please bear with us. Ah, perhaps you can simply tell us, yes or no. What you did—was it done in the regular, acceptable way?"

Shiela's mother struggled up, her eyes snapping. "Bishop, this child had sex for the first time. Do you expect her to be knowledgeable about all that? Isn't that right, Sheila?"

Shiela looked at her mother, her mouth slightly open. "Mom, I'm a grown up woman. I know quite a bit about a lot of things."

Mike Walle shot up like a night watchman hearing a noise in the dark. "You mean this wasn't the first man?"

Sheila turned to the Bishop. "This court was convened for the purpose of initiating a sequence of repentance. What does it matter what has happened in my past? All of us have past experiences for which we've repented. I'm not saying I've had sex with other men, but it seems irrelevant."

"Well, it's relevant to us if this type of behavior is habitual," Brother Walle said cooling a bit.

Bishop Sanders broke in again. The court was definitely straying from the manual. "Okay, all of you have good points. This is a court of love. Let's all remember that fact. Now, Sheila...ah...Sister Smith, just tell me, did you perform unnatural sex acts?"

Shiela shook her head, irritation showing.

"Have you had sex before?"

Sheila shook her head ever so slightly, flushing darkly.

"Okay, thank you. The time is getting late." Turning to Shiela's parents, the bishop invited them to say something, if they wished. Sheila's mother shook her head quickly and looked down.

Sheila's father got up. Raised a farmer, his rough, powerful body seemed out of place in the office. His wrinkled blue suit had seen a lot of Sunday pews. His weathered face and hands spoke of a love of the outdoors. He was known as a man who loved his children.

"Sheila's my daughter. She's a good gal. She's always been...my bright spot." He paused, groping for words. "Of course I'm upset about this whole thing, but I think I can understand how it must'a happened. I forgive 'er. As their daddy, I know when my kids are doin' what's right. She is, now. She's repented, far as I can tell. I love her, and I forgive...and I'll forget it, too. That's all I got to add, Bishop. Thank you."

Bishop Sanders thanked him for his counsel and said he was satisfied with the proceedings. He invited Sheila, her parents, and the clerks to wait in the foyer. When the room was cleared, he and his counselors knelt in prayer, and then sat around the bishop's desk.

"It's my responsibility to decide," the bishop began. "I must weigh the evidence, issue the verdict, and make the decisions. It's my job as bishop. But, I'd like your counsel. Brother Walle, what do you think?"

Mike was not as confident as before, but he stuck with his first impressions. "It's an open and shut case...I think," he said, a slight hint of doubt in his voice. "She's committed one of the most serious crimes a non-priesthood holder can commit. I say, excommunicate her. It will be the best action we can take because it will require sincere repentance on her part. She will suffer humiliation, but she will be stronger for it. I don't think she's exhibited sincere humility and sorrow yet. Excommunication will shock her into the proper attitude. That's my counsel...I guess."

Bishop Sanders was aware of the doubt in Mike's voice. He wondered what the blue box would say. "And you, Brother Petty?" the bishop asked, turning.

"Look, Bishop, I'm sorry for my question. I don't know what came over me...anyway, I think you might want to disfellowship her. Her repentance seems real to me. Disfellowshipment will be 'sack cloth and ashes' enough. And, another thing, I've known her parents since I was a kid. I think you ought to go easy on Sheila for her parents sake. They're wonderful people. Those are my feelings."

The bishop nodded. "Well, thank you. I'll consider what you've said with the rest of the information we've got. I'd like to be left alone for a few moments. Could you step out with the others for a little while?" As they left, he slid the drawer open and stared at the blue machine. All eight lights glowed, showing that the machine had heard and correctly stored the input from each person in the room, just as intended. Everyone's thoughts, beliefs, motivations, and feelings were stored in the machine's memory chips.

All that was required now was to ask its central processing unit to evaluate each person's input. The bishop reached for the control switch, but then hesitated. He sat in deep thought for a moment. A tiny bead of sweat appeared just above his eyebrow. Finally, a slight smile crossed his lips. Clicking the machine off, he closed the drawer and got down on his knees.

# Chapter 11

## The Mouth of Dark Canyon

*To have doubted one's own first principles is the mark of a civilized man.* -- Oliver Wendall Holmes

*Have you ever thought you heard someone only to turn and see no one there? Or seen something that turned out to be something else? Our senses often disappoint us. On the other hand, our senses can also be unexpected pathways to deep and hidden knowledge. In fact, what is the limit of our vision? our listening ability? our ability to feel? What is required to enjoy their full potential? And where do our sensory abilities end and our extra sensory gifts begin?*

During the spring of 1958, my best high-school buddy, Jim, and I traveled Dark Canyon, a little-known desert side-canyon of the Colorado River in southeastern Utah. No good maps were available in those days, but uranium hunters and cow punchers knew something about the area, and Jim's dad told us it was worth seeing.

It was a clear, blue, and cold Saturday evening when my brother stopped the jeep at the headwaters of Dark Canyon. Traveling north and west forty-five miles would bring us to the mouth of Dark Canyon in the cataracts of the Colorado River. We would meet my brother rafting down the Colorado on the following Saturday and float to Hite Ferry.

Our trek began at 8,700 feet. An icy stream of melted snow led through sparse pine, still-barren oak brush, and new spring grass poking up through last-year's matted, gray grass. We followed animal tracks where possible, but mostly we broke trail as we went. To be precise, Jim broke trail and I followed. The son of a rancher raised for twelve years in nearby Blanding, Jim had a pleasant, no-nonsense outlook on life, and felt completely at home in the wilderness.

This trip was different than any I had ever been on. I had been a spectator up to that point--reading about nature but never really immersing myself in it, dreaming adventure but content to watch it on TV, occasionally thinking deep thoughts about life, death, and love, but mostly accepting what I read and heard from others. I was a little unsure of my place in life--but I knew I was a young Mormon with access to all the answers. And I knew what I wanted: college, mission, money, girl-friends, career, home, family, and a sure testimony of the gospel, something that had eluded me so far.

As we hiked down the canyon I quickly realized there were no signs of recent human life--no footprints, old cans, or paper; no old fire pits; no roads or trails. There was nothing to indicate any prior human presence. Except, of course, for the Ancient Ones--the Anasazi. The side canyons were filled with silent wind-swept cliff dwellings, vivid reminders that this had been their land hundreds of years before.

Each day we visited the abandoned but still-intact cliff dwellings. I knew they had been vacant for centuries, but the pottery shards, the corn cobs, the manos and matates, the hardened handprints in the mud--all these spoke plainly of Indian life as it might have been. After the climb up the cliff, while Jim looked around, I would rest in the shade and conjure up visions of what life must have been like for the Anasazi. I could see men and women cooking, eating, talking, working, and playing with children. After a while, Jim would come and sit with me. Our visits always closed on the unanswerable questions: What did these ancient people think about? Did they love each other? What were their laws? What did they say to each other? Why were they here? What did they believe? Who was their God? Their prophets? Did God answer their prayers? Where did they fit in the plan of salvation? But Jim got bored of the unanswerable and I invariably grew tense and uneasy in a way I couldn't quite comprehend.

As the days passed and as we dropped deeper into the canyon, we watched steep red cliffs rise high into the sky above us, literally confining us to the canyon-bottom. I felt that we were totally isolated from the world and its people. It felt good, but it made me nervous, too. I had always relied on others. Relying on myself seemed frightening.

On Tuesday evening, our third night out, as the moon burst into the canyon, Jim asked me if I was homesick. I didn't really know what to say. It was a sensitive question and I hated to appear weak. Jim seemed so sure, so strong.

"No, not homesick, and not lonely either. You're here, and a great guy to be with," I offered. "But I'm feeling 'alone.' The peace, the lack of people, the quiet--these are all making me think and ask questions about the way I really feel about myself. I've been kind of quiet. Sorry."

Dark Canyon was the ultimate trip into aloneness. Jim and I enjoyed each other's company, but I found myself fascinated by solitude, and by the chance to wander about in the brushy bottom land, alone, in the midnight-like quiet. In modern life, background noises never cease their intrusion on our ears and minds. When we manage to get into a quiet place, we hear a buzzing in our ears--warning signs of overuse, even abuse, of our senses. It took a few days for my ears to adjust to the quiet. In Dark Canyon, we heard nothing but ourselves and natural sounds. After a few days, both of us noticed a new ability to hear with greater sensitivity. I could easily hear the call of the jay miles away, the sound of its wings beating against the air as it flew overhead. Hearing the unhearable, I seemed to fly with it. I marveled at the sound of the breeze in the canyon far ahead--its source endless and eternal. The night-time howl of a coyote somewhere in the canyon seemed oddly familiar. Listening and thinking, I somehow recognized his sadness.

When Jim and I were separated, I could track him by his noise--cracking branches, footfalls, and his quiet humming and whistling. Our noise seemed occasionally a sacrilege. How long had it been since clumsy human sounds had violated the sanctity of Dark Canyon? Yet, in spite of my awareness of myself as an intruder, I felt something in the canyon welcoming me.

On Thursday night, our fifth night, we camped in a lonely glen at the mouth of Lost Canyon, a deep and desolate side canyon. The afternoon sky was overcast, the birds strangely quiet. A soft cold breeze fluttered the blue-green leaves of a large, old cottonwood which lay across the now-widened stream bed. I wondered if the ancient tree had seen many humans before. John Wesley Powell surely passed this tree about a hundred years ago. But of course the Anasazi left the area more than 700 years ago, long before the cottonwood sprouted in the sandy bank.

After dinner, we decided to explore the mouth of Lost Canyon. In no hurry, we wandered up the canyon, enjoying the sparse desert sweet peas, snake grass, prickly pear cactus flowers, the on-again, off-again stream, (continued next page) red and tan cliff colors, jutting rocks, the strange calls and echoes of solitary frogs, and of course the quiet of twilight. Far up the canyon, we could see rain clouds and darkness.

"Do you think it will rain?" Jim asked, hinting to a fear of a flash flood.

"Flash floods don't occur in the Spring...do they?" I replied, not really confident.

Before long, the canyon sloped up abruptly. We scrambled up a rocky slide that ended at a fifteen foot sandstone cliff, which stretched in a semi-circle across the canyon. At its center, a small crack in the rock allowed us to chimney up. Jim went first and I followed. He was just about to the top when an awesome roaring noise cascaded down the canyon above us.

"Flash flood!" Jim yelled. Panic and the awful feeling of complete helplessness hit me. My mind was a firestorm. My eyes darted here and there down the rocky slope. Suddenly, I saw, for an instant, a short dark man. He was standing at the bottom of the slope, arms folded.

Amazingly the noise died away.

"It was thunder, I guess," Jim said, his voice high pitched. We chimneyed on up and sat down to think about the experience.

I kept looking down the slope, searching for the man I had seen. No one. "Did you see anyone . . . down there just a moment ago?" I asked. The words sounded utterly ridiculous.

"What?" Jim was confused. "No, did you?"

"I don't know. I thought so. My mind must've been playing tricks on me."

The rain reached us during the night. In my tent I watched drop after drop run down the outer nylon, and my mind went over the evening's experience. I struggled for more details about the man--but they wouldn't come. Just a man standing at the bottom of the slope, arms folded. Finally, I concluded the trauma must have set off a short-circuit in my mind. Rain drops followed each other hypnotically, running down the slope of the tent, one chasing the other, until sleep intervened.

Before noon on Friday, we reached the mouth of Dark Canyon. My brother wasn't due until Saturday. Jim and I spent a lazy afternoon washing, eating, swimming, and sun worshipping. At an elevation of 4,700 feet, the weather was much warmer. We had dropped almost 4,000 feet and now we were at least sixty miles from the nearest human settlement. It was almost over, but the trip seemed somehow incomplete. Questions about myself and life had come out of the cliffs and were hanging about like hungry dogs.

After dinner I left Jim by the fire and headed up a steep little side canyon to the southwest. It had no name that we knew of and didn't go far. In about half a mile, it narrowed to a small, sandy circular box, about thirty yards across. The solid cliffs on three sides stretched into the sky like the walls of a tall temple. I laid down on the soft sand and stared up at the clouds moving from left to right across the sky. The movement made me dizzy. I closed my eyes to restore my equilibrium, feeling peaceful and a little drowsy.

I heard footsteps somewhere down the canyon. Jim must be feeling lonely, I thought, propping myself up on an elbows. "Hey! I thought you weren't coming," I called out, anticipating the pleasure of sharing the amphitheater with him.

Around the canyon wall stepped a dark short man--the same man I had seen last night in Lost Canyon. Startled, I sat straight up. Who was it? Why was he following us? I felt for the knife in my pocket. It was there.

"Howdy," I said nervously. "It's a surprise to see anyone up here."

"Yes," he said. "It is."

I didn't recognize his accent. "We haven't seen anybody all week," I said. "Did you come up from the Colorado River?"

"No, not this time," he said.

"I saw you last night--up Lost Canyon. That was you, right?" I asked, now looking past him for a possible path of flight.

"Yes, it was I," he replied. He squatted in the sand in front of me, about twelve feet away. We said nothing for a moment. Then in one relaxed movement, he stretched out on the sand, hands behind his head, his gaze on the sky. He was wearing khaki pants and shirt, brown leather boots, and a hemp belt. I guessed him to be about 5 feet tall, 110 pounds, and 30 years old. His eyes were brown, his hair black, and his skin dark. His black beard was several days old and sparse like mine. Brown spots with long hairs blemished his cheek and forehead. I noticed his teeth were quite worn and several were missing. He carried nothing--no pack, no water, no walking stick, and no obvious weapons.

"What are you doing in the canyon, camping?" I asked.

"No, I live here," he said, shifting to turn directly toward me.

"Really!" I said, genuinely surprised. "Living where? We've seen no signs of anyone living along the canyon. Do you have a boat down on the river?"

"No, no boat. I live back in the place you call Young's Canyon."

"Right. The side canyon. We explored it Wednesday. That's a beautiful place. I'd live there too if I had to live in the canyons. But, we saw nothing--just the springs, the stand of tress, the waterfall, and a few cliff dwellings. Are you way up near the headwaters? And, what do you do there, anyway?"

"I live with my family. My home is about 30 minutes up Young's, in the four room dwelling on the north face by the waterfall. We just live there, that's all. You came to our house."

"What!? But how? There's no food . . . and . . . ." Fright pushed me to my feet. I looked down at the man. His eyes seemed friendly and warm.

"You're Indian, right?" I blurted out.

"Yes, I am." He sat up, looking squarely in my eyes. "But I'm from another time and place. An older, different place. I want to answer a few questions for you."

I stood still thinking frantic thoughts.

"I'm not crazy," he said softly, almost tenderly. "And neither are you. Go ahead, ask your questions."

I sat again, plopping heavily into the sand, unable to speak. My God, I thought, is this a religious experience? A dream? A hallucination? One of Jim's pranks?

He spoke again with a serene quality of love in his voice. "Please, ask your questions."

The man's kindness, his sincerity, his simpleness, and his care calmed me at once. Suddenly it seemed that I had known him all my life. "Okay," I said with my last vestige of doubt. "But I think . . . this is weird, isn't it?"

"Maybe."

"Well, okay. Aah, what do you think I should know?"

He smiled. "That's a good question. First you must know that God has the answers to your questions. Another is to know that you can find the answers yourself."

"What? How do I find these answers."

"By doing what you have been doing all week--removing worldly influences, exercising your senses, seeking to see your most innermost thoughts and true motivations, looking for the origins of your feelings, breaking through the crust that overlays your soul, dipping into and drinking from the font of faith."

I leaned back a little and looked at the cliffs and the sky. The shadows of the westward cliffs had climbed high on the east walls. Already, the cliff swallows had returned to their nests. It would be dark in a few more minutes. Suddenly I struggled with a deepening darkness inside.

He looked at me with kindness.

"I hope you won't mind," I said It seems so hard." I looked around nervously and picked up some sand. "I'm frightened by what I've seen in myself this week. I see weakness, hypocrisy, and opposition. A coward, and more. I am filled with doubts and evil questions." I wondered why I was telling this stranger all this. I certainly wouldn't have told Jim, my best friend.

"No question is evil," he said. "You may have seen these things in yourself, but they are not the real you. These things are only surface smudges which must be eventually wiped away. You are the creation of God, created through his love, and as such you are eternal, immortal, and ultimately a perfect creation. Look deeper."

My mouth went dry, as if suddenly filled with sand. "There is so much anxiety in these thoughts...and feelings." I stopped, my voice cracking.

"As you probe deeper into your feelings and motivations, and as you discover their origins, and remove those which scar the soul, you will experience peace. You will acquire eternal knowledge, and that will bring tranquility," he said.

I looked closely at this Indian. The soft silence filled the little canyon. "Who are you?" I finally managed.

"I am a friend . . . and a messenger," he said. "Do not disbelieve." His face seemed completely open. I could not look away from his dark, clear eyes. "Please, ask your questions--the ones you've been asking up there in the cliffs," he said, pointing high to the top of the sandstone pillars.

I managed to look down at my hands all red, sweaty, and spotted with sand. "Well, what about God? Does he really exist? Does he communicate with us? Is he a man?"

"Yes, He exists and He communicates. He can appear in any form He wants--a man, a woman, a star, the wind, even the river." He gestured in the direction of the Colorado.

"If you are right it means the Mormon Church is not true," I said. "We believe God is a man."

"Wrong. The Mormon Church is true. It is eternal. It is God's creation."

"How can that be?" I asked, confused.

"It is true for all those who have faith that it is," he said. "All God's creations are true."

"What?"

"It doesn't matter. Just accept that the Mormon Church is God's creation. In that sense, it is true."

"Please, I don't understand," I said, squirming. I felt confused--worse, embarrassed.

"All through history, in all parts of the world, God has established the seeds of truth. The Israelites, the Nephites, the Jaradites, everyone has
started with God's truths. But more importantly, religious truths can't flourish unless people have faith in them. President McKay is the Lord's prophet for his people mainly because you have faith that he is."

I felt adrift and grabbed hard for a straight answer. "Hey, look, is the Mormon Church the one and only true church upon the face of the earth, or not?" I was talking louder than I meant to and I honestly think any answer would have been sufficient. A simple "no" would have been as good as "yes."

"Yes, if you have that faith."

I was strangely comforted despite the further confusion. "I'm unsure of where all this leaves me. What does God expect from *me* ?" I asked.

"Live according to your beliefs. Be faithful. Fundamental righteousness is based on adherence to what you know to be right. You have been endowed with fundamental righteous understandings, ideals. Try to live by those ideals." He paused, searching for a final thought. "As God's creation, you have the things you need--right within yourself--to solve the dilemmas of life. Try to have faith in yourself."

He stood up and looked at the sky for a long moment, and then made a strange broad gesture toward the zenith with his right arm. He moved forward, leaned down, and almost touched my cheek with his hand. "I'd better be on my way," he said. He turned and started down the darkening canyon.

I stared after him for a few seconds. "Hey, wait!" I called. "What about ...." But he was already well ahead. "Wait a minute!" I struggled up out of the warm sand.

He went out of sight, weaving in and out of the dark shadows of sandstone. Running, I tried to catch him, but never did. Eventually, I came panting into the mouth of the canyon, where Jim was standing in the flicker of the camp fire.

"What's up?" Jim asked. "Afraid of the dark?"

"Did you see a man go by?" I asked.

"Not again?" he laughed, but with kindness.

"I'll tell you about it later," I said turning to my tent.

And later I did.

## Chapter 12

## First Impressions of a Salt Lake Landmark

*Doubt is pain too lonely to know that faith is his twin brother.*
— Kahil Gibran

*Note: Life is diversity. One person loves flowers; another hates pollen. You hear music; I hear noise. Some believe easily while others doubt easily; some require sensory evidence while others can accept by faith. No two people react to a thing in the same way. This story was written before the Great Salt Lake rose to record levels. Perhaps the moral is that changes can occur even when they are completely unexpected.*

I don't like to fly—in fact I don't even like to think about flying. For me, boarding a plane is like walking alone into a dark chapel at night—it makes me nervous. So when I fly, I do everything possible to keep my mind off what's happening to the plane. Conversation with fellow passengers distracts my mind from dangerous thoughts.

On a recent flight to Denver, I was seated between two young men.

Like ripe peas in a pod, we filled all of one side of Row 7. The flight was full and the weather a little blustery—a typical October afternoon.

And of course I was nervous. "Is Salt Lake your home?" I asked the man in the aisle seat just before takeoff.

"No, we're from Colorado Springs," he said, smiling and nodding his head toward the man at the window. His crisp New England accent and well-bred demeanor contrasted with his casual, western clothes. I was relieved that he was friendly.

"What brought you boys to Salt Lake? And how long were you here?" These are what I call "copper" questions—they lead either to the "golden" ones, or to a discussion of the copper mine for those not inclined to church conversation.

"We just came over to sightsee, and to go through the ... Salt Lake Temple," he said, hesitating on the last three words.

"Don't worry—I'm LDS, too," I said. "I go often." We shook hands in a brotherly way.

As the plane lifted off, I learned more about my traveling companions. They were brothers, John on the aisle and Bill at the window, aged twenty-four and twenty-six, originally from New Hampshire. Both had recently graduated from Yale University; neither was married; and both worked for companies near Denver—John as a civil engineering, Bill as an organizational psychologist. Their father was a minister, so their growing-up years had been filled with Christian activities—they had been choir boys, alter assistants, the works. Conversion to Mormonism a year ago in Hartford had been surprisingly easy, just before their dual graduations. And now they had made their maiden journey to the Mormon Mecca ... and it had been their first trip to the temple.

At the mention of the temple, there was another uneasy hesitation.

"We also went to the Great Salt Lake," John added awkwardly. He brushed back his blond hair which fell just to the collar of his red plaid cowboy shirt. He looked like a tall Robert Redford, I thought. But like many engineers, his pocket hosted a row of mechanical pencils. The dichotomy of a Robert Redford nerd entered my mind, but I quickly dismissed it.

"Really? What did you think of it?" I asked.

A pause. "The Great Salt Lake or the Salt Lake Temple?"

"The Great Salt Lake," I answered quickly. Talking about the temple is like talking about flying—it makes me nervous. And, casual conversations about either are impossible. Worse, *anything* might pop out of the mouths of two novice temple-goers. Planes are occasionally hit by lightning, and I didn't want to provide any extra incentive.

"Well, it was very interesting," John said, turning first to look at me, then stretching his neck to look over at his brother. Bill's silent expression betrayed a friendly disagreement. "*I* really liked it," John concluded, leaning back.

This emphasis his cue, Bill turned from the window and reluctantly volunteered, "I guess *I* was disappointed, all in all." I guessed Bill to be about six foot six, and less than 200 pounds. He was big, but his voice was soft, hard to hear over the airplane noise.

"Why were you disappointed?" I asked, surprised. How could anyone be disappointed with such a well-established Utah landmark? I wondered. It was like someone saying they didn't like Alta, the Hotel Utah, Mirror Lake, or Zion's National Park.

"Well, I'd heard so much about it, and I guess I really built it up in my mind." Bill paused and looked out the window. Sunlight shone warm on his brown sports coat. Unlike John, he was dressed in a white shirt and tie. His hair, blond like his brother's, was thinning in front—a shiny spot was showing through in the sunlight. He looked like a thoughtful person, but at this moment there was anguish showing on his tanned face. "Look, it was different from what I thought it would be, that's all," he finished, sitting back with a finality. He folded his arms and continued looking out the window.

"Okay," I said. "Don't worry about what I'll think. But, really, I'm curious about why you were so disappointed."

Bill seemed pleased that someone was interested in his feelings. "Okay, I think I'd like to tell you. First, you should know that I love swimming. My father spent years teaching us to swim. It's been a big thing in my life—college swim team, scuba diving, the works. So the first disappointment for me was the lake's shallowness." His hands went down in the sign of something low.

"But I don't like to be in over my head," John said.

"Well, it was far from that," Bill responded to his brother. Leaning forward to see us better, he said, "John and I put on our suits and literally ran into the water. That felt so good we headed for deeper water. We walked for twenty minutes—and the water was still only at our thighs!"

"We never did find any really deep water in two hours of wading," John admitted. "But that didn't bother me."

"It's never been famous because it was deep," I agreed, trying not to sound defensive.

John continued, "We finally just sat back in the water. I enjoyed that. It was quiet and peaceful, the sun was shining, people around were friendly, and a warm breeze was blowing. Best of all, the water was buoyant. I was amazed how it could lift me up. I really felt great!" He leaned back and closed his eyes, obviously enjoying the memory.

"I enjoyed the peace and quiet, too," Bill agreed. "But the water's buoyancy—actually its saturated heaviness—bothered me. The water kept pushing me back to the surface, tipping me over, making me lose my balance. I couldn't really get into it." Bill loosened his neck tie a little. His neck was slightly sunburned. I noticed he wore a scuba diver's wrist watch.

"Did you try swimming?" I asked.

Bill's face was intense. "That place is something else! Everytime I started to swim, I got salt in my eyes. The pain was awful. Even with my background, real swimming was impossible."

"But salt adds savor, Bill," John said. "Think what life would be without it!"

"I like salt fine," Bill said, irritated at John's mild joke. "But not when it's heavy and oppressive. Not when it keeps me from enjoying the water."

The conversation was interrupted by the captain on the intercom: "Good morning, folks. We're climbing through 10,500 feet on our way to our assigned altitude of 33,000 feet. Now, off to your right you can see the Great Salt Lake, and to our left is the beautiful downtown Salt Lake City ..."

Everyone strained to see through the windows. Yes, the lake stretched off to the western horizon, its blue and green bands of water gleaming like polished metal in the afternoon sunlight. To the east we could see the city and its temple, surrounded by the downtown skyscrapers like strong young servants around an old master.

"Look at the lake." John observed almost with reverence. "It's beautiful like the ocean—powerful, invigorating, inspiring, full of life and hope."

Bill scratched his eyebrow and sighed. "That just the surface. Actually, the lake is just the opposite of the ocean—weak, uncreative, and sterile. You know, its almost completely devoid of life. The only thing that can live in its waters are brine shrimp—helpless, mindless creatures eternally treading water."

"But birds—beautiful seagulls—live on the lake, too." John protested.

"But they have to fly elsewhere for real nourishment," Bill said.

John responded, "But they always return to the lake. Despite its shortcomings, it somehow provides protection and comfort—a place of refuge. You remember how carefree they seemed, soaring over the lake."

Bill nodded. "It's a deep dilemma for him," John said to me. He reached over and touched Bill tenderly on the leg. Bill's smile thanked John for his understanding.

"I've never heard anyone talk about it like this before," I observed, speaking to no one in particular. Bill's intense disappointment made me nervous. It had the sudden depth of a cold mountain lake after you've fallen out of a canoe.

Fortunately, I'm a good floater. The time had come to change the subject.

For the rest of our flight we talked about the weather, the football season, and business. Dinner was served, the plane landed without crashing, and we said a quick goodbye. I felt sorry that Bill had such a troubling first impression. But he'll get over it. It's just a matter of not thinking too much about it.

# Chapter 13

# Faith Run Amok

*Note: A metaphor is figure of speech in which one element or situation is assigned the attributes of another, for instance calling old age the "autumn of life." The term "faith to move mountains" has come to mean the power to influence events through great faith and understanding.*

*We are urged to strengthen our faith. To what extent could a person develop faith and its attendant power? The central figure of this fantasy possesses a strange power to literally influence events through faith run amok.*

"What'll we tell the paramedics?" I asked Jane, pointing to the four men who lay groaning on the floor, their faces swollen like beaten prizefighters.

Jane shook her head. "I don't know," she said. "Just say they were being animals." Jane's a sensible and straight-forward person.

Jane and I had been having a quiet salad at The Rest, an off-campus restaurant, when four campus jocks pushed their way in, laughing, punching, strutting for the girls. They took a table next to ours. Jane and I had only an hour before my next class and her next shift at the library. I had been looking forward to a quiet hour.

All those empty tables and they have the nerve to sit right by us, I grumbled to myself. "Look at those beasts. I can't tell whether they're gorillas, jackasses, or pigs," I whispered to Jane.

"Speaking of metaphors," Jane said, "collectively, they'd make a good living metaphor for 'obnoxious.'"

"Absolutely," I answered. "By the way, have you ever seen a metaphor become an actuality?"

"No. I don't know what you are talking about."

"Well, it sometimes happens to me...particularly if I'm feeling very emotional. For example, a classic metaphor is the rose, representing young love—you know, fragrant, beautiful, and inviting...but with thorns, and withering if not nurtured. Well, last week I met a girl in the Student Union who really turned me on. I kept thinking of a rose as we talked. Well, I went to the john, and when I came back, she was gone. But there was a single red rose on the chair where she had been! Isn't that a fantastic story!"

Jane response was an annoyed yawn. "Just don't think of me as your 'bosom buddy', okay?" I had struck a nerve.

We turned our attention to the circus side show at the jock's table next to ours. Mountains of food were being delivered to the clowns: spare ribs, coleslaw, green salads, pitchers of beer, bread, shrimp, ham, potatoes, raw and cooked vegetables, pies, and cakes.

"Four guys can't eat all that, can they?" Jane whispered.

"You don't know jocks very well," I replied. "They revel in creating a metaphor for gluttony."

The four stuffers suddenly switched into high gear as if motivated by an impending famine. Bread, butter, ribs, and potatoes disappeared, washed down with guzzles of beer. Forks were too slow and were soon displaced by flying fingers, wet and sticky. As the food diminished, the waitress invariably appeared with fresh rations.

"Hogs at a trough," I offered.

The gluttons leaned heavily against the table, sitting on the edge of their chairs, occasionally rising to snatch something out of reach. Their machine mouths chewed steadily to the beat of their hearts. Without emotion, their eyes scanned the table for the next mouthful.

"What kind of living metaphor do we have now?" Jane asked.

"It looks like 'suicide' to me," I said, turning with disgust.

Jane grabbed my arm. "Look!" She said nodding nervously in their direction.

I stared. The four jocks were furiously stuffing food into their mouths. They seemed in a kind of food panic. Slowly, they stood, in unison, and leaned heavily toward the center of the table, feeding their themselves all the while. Their faces were bloated and swollen with food but their eyes continued empty of emotion.

In a few seconds their heads were almost touching over the center of the table, each bobbing and weaving in its feeding frenzy.

"They'd better watch out. Somebody's going to get hurt," I said nervously to Jane. "Hey, Miss!" I yelled to the waitress, hoping to somehow defuse this bomb before it exploded.

Immediately, their four heads met over the table and stuck together like magnets, cheek against bloated cheek, nose flat against nose, forehead to forehead, ear to ear. It was as if four unseen gorillas were lifting and pushing each man's head from behind.

Shortly, we heard gasping and sucking noises, as their airways were blocked shut. Noses, cheekbones, and jaws popped and cracked as the four heads merged into a single greasy, sweaty mass. Their bodies, innocent bystanders below, began to shake with pain and terror.

"Think of something!" Jane shouted. "Make up another metaphor . . . something for survival!" .

"My God, do you really think that the metaphors . . . ?" My mouth fell open and I sat back in my chair, stunned. "Yeah . . . MITOSIS, MITOSIS!" I shouted.

With a sucking sound the heads divided from the central mass one by one. the heads divided from the central mass, sending each jock to the floor, moaning and groaning in pain and fright.

After the paramedics came and the four were safely on their way to medical care, Jane and I sat again, drained.

"This is frightening!" Jane exclaimed, shaking her head. "Can you explain how you create these living metaphors?"

My mind was an empty bag. "No. I'd better see the bishop."

# Chapter 14

# Helping Those With Religious Questions and Doubts

*To some it is given to know that Jesus Christ is the Son of God. To others it is given to believe on their words, that they also might have eternal life if they continue faithful.*-- (D&C 46:13-14)

*Note: Versions of this essay have appeared in the* Association of Mormon Counselors and Psychotherapists (AMCAP) Journal, Exponent II, *and* Counseling II - A Guide to Helping Others, *(Deseret Book, 1985)*

## INTRODUCTION

Mormonism is known, among other things, for its emphasis on personal conviction and strong testimony. Members are expected to receive a manifestation or confirmation that the essentials of the gospel are true. Partly because of this expectation, Latter-day Saints with unresolved religious questions and uncertainties may experience agonizing introspection, emotional difficulties, and even self-imposed alienation.

One aspect of the problem is what Mormon psychologist Frances Lee Menlove described as the unruffled Mormon syndrome. The unruffled Mormon is an ideal: A completely fulfilled and integrated Latter-day Saint, untroubled by doubts and questions which afflict others. Oblivious to the pain and probings of other truth-seekers, this member is secure in the ability to understand all religious issues. (*Dialogue* 1:1, 1967)

Although many Mormons live comfortably close to the unruffled ideal, others have found themselves unable to achieve this serenity. Attempts to fit into this mold frequently create a number of problems. For example, those who repress their natural urge to question so they can maintain an unruffled image may settle for the appearance of belief in place of actual conviction. Over a period of time, such self-deception can create emotional conflict and foster feelings of guilt and hypocrisy. They may confide: "I'm living a lie." "What's wrong with me? I can't live up to the expectations of others." "I feel so guilty—the Lord must hate me."

Latter-day Saints struggling for conviction are often caught in an endless cycle of attempts and failures to achieve the perceived perfection of the unruffled state. These defeats can result in feelings of frustration, discouragement, unworthiness, or low self-esteem: "I've prayed and fasted but I still have questions. Why don't I get the same answers as others?" "I just can't accept a calling (go to the temple, etc.) while I have these nagging doubts." "I don't deserve blessings because I have uncertainties and questions inside."

Latter-day Saints desiring to discuss their questions and doubts often find communication difficult or impossible. With no chance to talk, emotional, spiritual, and intellectual growth are often stunted. Without meaningful discussion with fellow members, a person can feel alienated from the religious community, either through emotional withdrawal or loss of Church activity: "If I can't have the same assurance as others, I don't want to participate." "I can't talk to anybody about this." "If it weren't for the kids (my parents, my wife, my husband), I'd just quit it all."

Persons with unresolved doubts may experience marital conflicts, denial of reality, reduced ability to deal with feelings and emotions, reduced motivation to learn, and feelings of disorientation: "My wife keeps saying, 'Why can't you just believe? Why do you have to question everything?' She thinks I'm not trying, that I'm somehow unworthy of the blessings of a sure knowledge. Why can't she just understand that's the way I am?" "I'm a basket case. I can't get on with anything."

Religious doubt may arise at any age, but it is more typically seen during the years of intellectual maturation. Those desiring to help should be particularly sensitive to this problem among young adults, and especially among college students.

## PERSPECTIVES ON HELPING THOSE WITH DOUBTS

Many of the problems associated with religious questions and doubt grow out of misconceptions concerning the relationship of knowledge to faith and belief and their roles in our lives. I have found ten perspectives on the nature of religious conviction and commitment helpful to me as I have talked with struggling friends and loved ones. These perspectives can help them to see their circumstances in a more positive light and to pave the way to personal growth and emotional satisfaction.

1. Mormonism and society assign different meanings to "faith" and "belief."

Mormons often see belief and faith as synonymous, both being the natural result of learning truth. The scriptures often use the two words interchangeably. However, in our present day society, particularly in the sciences, the terms belief and faith have distinct, mutually exclusive meanings.

In the contemporary sense, belief is a mental state that tells us something is true because of experience, information, evidence, or authority. For example, if we flip a coin fifty times and tabulate the numbers of heads and tails, we are likely to believe from the evidence that each comes up about equally. Of course, no one person's interpretation of the evidence will prove satisfactory to everyone. A mother looks at a newborn baby and has sufficient evidence to believe in the existence of God. A biochemist looking at the same child may marvel at the power of evolution.

*Faith,* on the other hand, refers to a feeling, a *trust* in "the evidence of things not seen" (Heb. 11:1). Belief is learned; faith is evidence yet to be learned. Belief is what we really think; faith is what we are willing to accept in the absence of evidence.

The acceptance embodied in faith implies an active personal commitment. Thus, under these definitions, it is possible to question aspects of our religion, yet live the gospel by faith.

*Helping suggestion:* Accept the possibility that you both may be operating under different definitions as you discuss belief and faith. Define your terms to assure clear communication.

2. Doubting is not necessarily a rejection of God.

Again, it is important to recognize the multiple meanings of *doubt*. In its modern, constructive sense, it means to be unsettled in belief or opinion, to be uncertain or undecided. It implies a lack of information or evidence upon which to base a belief. Doubt, according to this usage, is an inevitable consequence of a maturing, inquiring mind and should be managed, not denied.

In contrast, the more traditional meaning of doubt is the notion of distrust or disloyalty. In a religious context, doubt is often associated with a rejection of God and a thankless denial of his goodness. Naturally, in this context, it has a negative connotation.

Helping Suggestion: Point out that those who are aware of differences of meaning can avoid being hurt (or avoid offending others) by choosing their words carefully and defining any likely-to-be misunderstood expressions.

3. "It is not permitted to know everything." —Horace.

We in the church often use the words, "I know" to describe our testimonies ("I know the Church is true.") This use of *know* usually means a strong belief or faith ("I intensely believe the Church is true," or "My faith is strong that the Church is true.")

"To know," in its modern, technological sense, is to have a clear understanding, or to be relatively sure. Knowledge is familiarity with or awareness of facts and evidence. But in mortality nothing can be known with perfection, only in degrees of confidence. While science and statistics have developed elaborate methods for testing, verifying, and strengthening the evidence upon which beliefs and knowledge are based, no test produces perfect knowledge. Furthermore, scientists themselves use faith when they rely on their own methods or unproven assumptions, or when confidence limits exist, however small.

Helping Suggestion: Show that since no one can claim perfect knowledge, it is only reasonable to expect a degree of uncertainty in this mortal life. Discuss the different uses of the words "knowledge" and "to know."

4. Most Mormons wonder about things religious.

Wondering is a common and natural reaction to all but the most commonplace information. What Mormon, for example, hasn't had one or more of the following thoughts cross his or her mind at some time?

- Why would God command Adam and Eve not to eat of the Tree of Knowledge of Good and Evil? Nephi to kill Laban? Joseph Smith to practice polygamy?
- Did Joseph Smith truly translate gold plates and papyri? find the Garden of Eden?
- Is my bishop (father, husband, stake president, leader) really inspired in this call (decision, release, judgment)?

A popular but misguided approach to dealing with such wondering is to blame Satan or the weakness of the questioner.

Helping Suggestion: Point out that wondering is natural, and that unless sin is clearly involved, guilt and repression are unnecessary and only serve to cause pain or to divert attention away from the real issues.

5. Everyone is a believer to some degree; our uncertainties vary in strength.

Latter-day Saints who are uncertain about particular tenets of the religion should not be hasty in applying negative labels to themselves. In time, such negative self-labeling will undermine self-esteem. Alma was right: A little belief is like a seed. Nourishment and care may produce a tall, strong Tree of Knowledge. But that takes faith, time, and work.

Helping Suggestion: Point out that varying strengths of belief in different facets of the gospel are not uncommon and are not the same as unbelief; indeed, it is highly unlikely that any two people will share exactly the same convictions on all issues. Help the person to see that he or she is an integral part of a diverse Church, rather than an outsider. Suggest prioritizing concerns about particular beliefs and faith. ("Which is a more important consideration, that Jesus is the Christ, or that coffee is included in the Word of Wisdom?")

6. Properly approached, questioning is a vital part of the learning process.

Having questions imply a desire to expand the information upon which beliefs are based. Mormonism celebrates intelligence as "the glory of God" (D&C 93:36), and proclaims that we are saved no faster than we gain knowledge. Obviously, such commitment to learning cannot be served by suppressing inquiries about the kingdoms of heaven and earth.

On the other hand, questions asked to challenge or accuse are not part of sincere inquiry. Suppose a Church member has trouble understanding why the Lord would command Nephi to kill Laban. How does he or she seek information and express true feelings without sounding distrustful, negative, or dissenting? Such threatening overtones can frequently be avoided by prefacing questions with honest statements of feelings: "I'm troubled by..." "It bothers me greatly, but I am skeptical of..." "My heart tells me..." "I feel anguish when I think about..." "Please don't misunderstand me; I am a committed, faithful member of the Church, but I have a question I'd like your opinion on..." "This is a question that has caused me a lot of turmoil. I want to talk to you because I respect you. I wonder if you could tell me what you think about (know about)...?" "I wonder if you've ever had the same question that's been running through my mind:..." "I haven't enough information yet to have a perfect knowledge of the issue, but here's what I believe (here's the evidence upon which I base my belief...)"

Helping Suggestion: Show that the pursuit of truth is rarely harmed by sincere questions made in the spirit of humble curiosity. Review with the person nonthreatening ways of asking questions. Encourage the person to be honest about his or her feelings.

7. The blessings of the gospel come through faithfulness and obedience; particular beliefs may vary within certain bounds.

Some Mormons assume that there is only one way to believe in Church doctrines. Quite to the contrary, a great deal of freedom exists on matters of belief in religious concerns. Joseph Smith reportedly said, "The most prominent difference in sentiment between the Latter-day Saints and sectarians was that the latter were all circumscribed by some peculiar creed, which deprived its members of the privilege of believing anything not contained therein, whereas the Latter-day Saints have no creed, but are ready to believe all true principles that exist" (HC 5:215).

Similarly, President Joseph F. Smith testified before the Congress of the United States that Latter-day Saints "are given the largest possible latitude of their convictions, and if a man rejects a message that I may give to him but is still moral and believes in the main principles of the gospel and desires to continue in his membership in the Church, he is permitted to remain." In the same setting, he observed:

"Members of the Mormon church are not all united on every principle. Every man is entitled to his own opinion and his own views and his own conceptions of right and wrong so long as they do not come in conflict with the standard principles of the Church. If a man assumes to deny God and to become an infidel we withdraw fellowship from him. But so long as a man believes in God and has a little faith in the Church organization, we nurture and aid that person to continue faithfully as a member of the Church though he may not believe all that is revealed." (*The Reed Smoot Hearings,* pp 97-98.)

*Helping Suggestion:* Show that questions and uncertainties concerning religion should not keep a person from participating in all facets of the gospel and need not prevent the person from full enjoyment of gospel blessings.

8. Not all information is correct; no source of information is complete.

No single source of information can exhaust the facts concerning any gospel issue. Furthermore, some sources are wrong and others are written to deceive. Still others are well-intentioned but misleading. Historical studies, for example, are subject to many limitations because they involve both the acquisition of sometimes scarce factual information and also the dubious process of correctly interpreting that information.

*Helping Suggestion:* Caution the person against jumping to conclusions based on inevitably inadequate information. Reemphasize the need for faith during the information-gathering and knowledge-development phases.

9. An individual can control his or her personal responses to questions and doubts.

Our basic emotions are largely unavoidable: we cannot avoid feelings of sadness when a friend dies; we cannot avoid feelings of joy when we are blessed; and we cannot avoid feeling troubled when we do not understand something important. On the other hand, we can *control* our reactions to our emotions, and we can *manage* our behavior. Control and positive management of difficult emotions are always helped by understanding the emotion--its origin, its reason for being, and its potential solutions.

A man's troubled response to doubt and questioning may result in part from the way he was reared. Suppose, for example, as a young boy he innocently asked, "Did Joseph really see God?" If his parent or teacher responded with horror, "Of course he did! How could you ask such a thing?" the child may have concluded that questions are unimportant or bad. As he grew to adulthood, he may have come to see skepticism and curiosity as defects. Personal doubts may have been seen as inappropriate temptations rather than challenges to be explored and investigated. Thus, leaders, teachers, and parents may have unwittingly planted the seeds of trouble years ago.

The person may also be influenced by local responses to perceived skepticism. The local community may foster guilt as a response to doubt and inculcate the notion that questioning is a sign of sin, slothfulness, or error. Such negative reactions represent the fears and weakness of individuals and are not part of the gospel.

Helping Suggestion: Help the person to understand his or her feelings and the local environment. Urge him or her to accept these conditions with patience and love while learning new ways to manage emotions associated with questions and doubts.

10. Religion has a spiritual component that is essential to the process of learning spiritual truths.

The quotation from the Doctrine and Covenants which opens this chapter, tells us that some are given to know and that others are given to believe on their words. We have no way of discerning in advance who will know and who will live by faith; nor do we know why the Lord has established such a system. We don't even know which of the two is more blessed. But we are told that to those who continue faithfully in the absence of knowledge, there is a promise of eternal life.

Religion has a spiritual dimension, sometimes called the supernatural or metaphysical, which cannot be explained by contemporary empirical methods. And we believe that a person's spirit and mind can be taught truths which cannot be learned otherwise. But such experiences require obedience, faith, and a sincere heart.

Helping Suggestion: Explore the possibilities of giving the spiritual side of life a better chance to succeed. Explore the possibility that the person's attitude, or personal sin, may be blocking spiritual learning methods.

## SPECIFIC THINGS TO DO

As in all helping activities, you need to show concern, nonjudgement, and understanding for the pain and difficulty the religious doubter may be experiencing. In addition, there are a number of practical suggestions (or challenges) you can offer the person:

- Look within, analyze feelings, and determine true beliefs; don't be afraid of what you find.
- Work to be worthy of building faith through obedience, prayer, study, and good works.

- Establish personal study programs to expand the information and evidence upon which your beliefs and knowledge are built.
- Give spiritual methods a chance.
- Seek help when needed and admit fallibility.
- Talk about questions in tactful, nonthreatening ways. Be willing to listen to the insights of others. Don't forget to express positive beliefs and levels of faith, too.

Finally, you should leave your friend or loved one with hope. James Francis Cooke said it best: "The most welcomed people of the world are never those who look back upon the bitter frustrations of yesterday, but those who cast their eyes forward with faith, hope, courage, and happy curiosity."

# Chapter 15

## Bibliographic Essay: What Some Great Thinkers Have Said about Faith

*In this section I list and briefly discuss books and articles on the subjects of faith, belief, doubt, reason, and knowledge that have been helpful to me. The list is not all inclusive, nor is it intended to represent the only important works.*

DISCUSSION. In each commentary, I have tried to represent not only the author's views but also the spirit with which he writes. I lean toward the views and styles of Fowler and Moreno, and perhaps some of that bias will show. In any event, I hope you feel the urge to obtain and read these works, and others. Here are some general conclusions:

I have observed some interesting phenomena as I have read these works on faith and reason. I will simply list them and let you compare them to your own conclusions:

Thinkers on contrasting sides of the spectrum (e.g., Tillich and

Talmage, Russell and Pratt) say a lot of the same things and often use the same arguments to prove widely different conclusions.

The most vigorous critics of faith acknowledge its usefulness and often become its defenders. Similarly, the most vigorous critics of reason depend on reason to make their points.

All authors write with admirable conviction; many use the universal "we," assuming that every person thinks, acts, and feels as they do.

Those who defend faith assume God is on their side. Those who defend reason assume God desires human beings to liberate, use, and depend on reason.

Those who use reason and rational thought to evaluate the human condition eventually increase the number of possible conclusions, never create certainty, and inevitably produce doubt. In doing so, they create the need for faith.

The very need to argue the benefits of faith vs. reason points up our inability to reconcile the two; *uncertainty* is the only outcome. Each person is then left to choose the amount of reason and faith appropriate for his or her needs.

The following commentaries are listed in approximate chronological order of publication.

## *JOSEPH SMITH*

From the Doctrine and Covenants; The History of the Church of Jesus Christ of Latter-day Saints (*DHC,* 7 vols.); *Lectures on Faith,* comp. Neal B. Lundwall (Salt Lake City; Bookcraft); and Ehat and Lyndon B. Cook, comps. and eds.; *The Words of Joseph Smith: The Contemporary Accounts of the Nauvoo Discourses of the Prophet Joseph,* (Salt Lake City, Bookcraft for BYU Religious Study Center, 1980)

Joseph Smith, first prophet and president of the Church of Jesus Christ of Latter-day Saints, was a prolific writer/speaker, and much of his most important work is found in modern-day scripture. Surprisingly, non-scriptural sources attributed to him mention little on the subjects of faith and belief, more on knowledge, and very little on doubt, skepticism, or reason. Perhaps as a dynamic leader, Joseph was more interested in the day-to-day management of the Church, in explaining doctrine and gospel applications, and in encouraging *knowing* over believing. Perhaps as a result of his personal experiences, Joseph believed a person could come to a knowledge of almost anything through study and personal revelation from God.

FAITH. In March 1842, Joseph wrote to an editor, John Wentworth describing the young Mormon Church. In the letter he included a thirteen-part statement of the doctrines of the Church—the "Articles of Faith." The fourth article states that the first four principles of the gospel are "faith in Jesus Christ, ... repentance, baptism, and ... the gift of the Holy Ghost."

Personal faith, according to teachings attributed to Joseph Smith, comes by hearing the word of God and through the testimony of the servants of God. (HC 3:379) He saw a spectrum of faith among men: "If a man has not faith to do one thing, he may do another; if he cannot remove a Mountain, he may heal the sick." (Ehat and Cook 1980, p. 191)

Faith, for Joseph, was not only a gift of God, but the source of God's gifts, the very reason for the existence of the gospel's fruits: "Because faith is wanting, the fruits are. No man has had faith without having some gift along with it. The ancients quenched the violence of fire, escaped the edge of the sword, women received their dead, etc. A man who has none of the gifts has no faith. Faith has been wanting . . . so that tongues, healings, prophecy, and all the gifts and blessings have been wanting." (HC 5:218)

FAITH AND THE PHYSICAL BODY. Joseph Smith, in an experience attributed to him, spoke of an act of faith as one which can literally tire the body. "A man who exercises great faith in administering to the sick, blessing little children, or confirming, is liable to become weakened. Elder Grant inquired of me the cause of my turning pale and losing strength last night while blessing children. I told him ... I strove with all the faith and spirit that would secure their lives upon the earth; and so much virtue went out of me ... that I became weak, from which I have not yet recovered." (HC 5:303)

BELIEF. Joseph Smith encouraged a diversity of intellectual beliefs. He once corrected the high council for calling up a man for erring in doctrine. Joseph wrote that he did not like the concept of a creed, which a man must believe or be asked out of the Church. "I want the liberty of believing as I please, it feels good not be to trammelled. It don't prove that a man is not a good man, because he errs in doctrine." (Ehat and Cook 1980, p.183-84)

KNOWLEDGE. Joseph Smith was the champion of knowledge: "In knowledge there is power. God has more power than all other beings, because he has greater Knowledge, and hence he knows how to subject all other beings to him." (Ehat and Cook 1980, pp 183) Joseph repeatedly taught that knowledge saves, and that no one can be exalted except by knowledge, but knowledge is only given as people are prepared for it. "The Lord deals with this people as a tender parent with a child, communicating light and intelligence and the knowledge of His ways as they can bear it."

In Joseph's scriptures (the Doctrine and Covenants), faith and belief are mentioned at least twenty times, primarily as they relate to faith in Jesus Christ and his gospel. Doubt and disbelief are mentioned seven times, light and knowledge, forty-five times--almost always exhorting the reader to obtain or receive knowledge.

For me, Joseph Smith emerges as a strong leader urging his followers to be believers, to be faithful, and above all, to be knowledgeable. This is a prophet of God who taught that the glory of God is intelligence; and he put his faith in a knowledgeable body of followers.

## *ORSON PRATT*

"True Faith," in *Lectures on Faith,* comp. by Neil B. Lundwall (Salt Lake City) Bookcraft.

A review of Orson Pratt's essay, "True Faith," the second part of the book *Lectures on Faith,* is included here as an interesting counterpoint to *The Will to Doubt* by Bertrand Russell. Each man represents opposing sides of the faith/reason spectrum--and yet they exhibit curious similarities. Pratt's essay is presented in a forceful, scholarly, and reasoned format, not unlike Russell's. Each uses similar arguments to prove different points about faith.

Faith, Pratt asserts, is not an abstract principle, separate and distinct from the mind, but is a definite state of the mind itself. "When the mind believes any subject, or statement, or proposition, whether correct or incorrect, it is then in possession of faith. To have faith is simply to believe" (p. 70). For Pratt, belief and faith are synonymous, often interchangeable in theory and usage.

Faith requires evidence, and Pratt is emphatic that without such evidence one cannot believe or have faith in anything. He acknowledges only two types of faith: *true* faith based on true evidence and *false* faith. A false faith originates when one believes in false evidence.

Fortunately, "faith in every word of God, whether ancient or modern, is always produced by evidence that is true, and calculated to give the greatest assurance to the mind" (p. 71). Since faith is based on evidence, faith's strength varies with the weight of evidence. Where evidence is doubtful, faith will be weak; where evidence is strong, faith
*(continued next page)*

will be strong; where there is no evidence to the contrary, then again faith should be strong. However, an exception to these rules can be found in minds where "judgement becomes so weak and beclouded ... and in minds so impaired or vitiated that the evidence ... produces no sensible impression on the mind" (p. 71). Pratt continues on for several long paragraphs describing various deceptive and false evidences, and the causes of impaired minds—false religious teachings.

Orson Pratt, following Joseph Smith's lead, says that faith is the source of action. Faithful acts or works parallel a person's faith. Idolatrous faith produces idolatrous works; faith in false doctrines leads to wicked practices; and "faith in a divine message or new revelation will lead to works in accordance with the requirements contained therein" (p. 73). The effect of a true and correct faith is a sincere and thorough repentance followed by baptism and confirmation by the Holy Ghost.

Faith alone, however, will not save men or women. Even faith and works are not enough unless they are of the "proper" kinds. Pratt proceeds, with admirable vigor, to explain the restoration and its place in assuring proper faith and works. (A single paragraph continues for over two pages. It's like listening to an excited man who never takes a breath, and it requires great courage on the part of the reader to begin the long journey.)

Like others, Pratt believes faith to be a gift of God. But God will not bestow this gift, even though "purchased for the man not by his own works, but by the blood of Christ" (p. 82). It, as well as other heavenly gifts, cannot be bestowed without works—" ... before he can receive and enjoy them he must exercise his agency, and accept them, ... and then only in God's own appointed way" (pp. 82-83). Pratt concludes his spirited explanation by describing the gift of faith as strictly contingent upon obedience to latter-day gospel laws, ordinances, and principles.

Pratt was probably writing to investigators of the Church, because much of the essay is typical of arguments probably encountered at early missionary meetings: "Reader, are you a believer or an unbeliever? Do signs follow you, according to the promise of Jesus? Have you ever cast out devils? Have you ever had faith to prevail against deadly poisons? If not, then you are not a gospel believer, and are included in the class which Jesus says shall be damned. Your condition is a fearful one, without the true faith, without hope, without salvation, exposed to the wrath which must fall upon unbelievers" (p. 92).

## WILLIAM JAMES

*The Varieties of Religious Experience,* (New York, Mentor Books, 1958)

William James is widely recognized as one of the great modern philosophical minds. *The Varieties of Religious Experience,* a compilation of lectures presented at the University of Edinburgh in 1902, has become a major force in religious literature.
Jacques Barzun, in a foreword written for the 1958 edition, suggests that "the reader will not find James a conventional scientist who used the facts of physiology or psychology to explain away the facts of religious life . . . As a student of religion he has illuminated a wonderful variety of recorded experiences by grouping, comparing, and analyzing them."
William James lived and wrote in an era pre-dating modern statistical methods. His findings, as such, are based on anecdotal evidence, and represent the conclusions of a single brilliant mind. However, I suspect he might, even today, use the same nonscientific methods because his major conclusion is that religion is ultimately a personal and metaphysical phenomenon, and thus is not easily studied through scientific, systematic methods.

James confines himself to the study of personal religion: "I . . . ignore the institutional branch entirely, to say nothing of the ecclesiastical organization, consider as little as possible the systematic theology and ideas about the gods themselves, and confine myself to personal religion pure and simple" (p. 41). Personal religion proves itself more fundamental than any other approach: "Churches, when once established, live at second-hand upon tradition; but the founders of every church owed their power originally to their direct personal communion with the divine" (p. 42). James defines personal religion as the feelings, the acts, and the experiences of individuals alone as they understand themselves and their relationship to God.

As for belief and faith in such a personal religion, James has a number of observations.

BELIEF AND HAPPINESS. Personally experiencing religion produce "wonderful inner paths to a supernatural kind of happiness." This happiness seem's proof to believers of the truth of their personal religion. When a belief makes a person feel happy, the person will inevitably adopt it, or acknowledge its veracity, or at least suggest that it ought to be true. And because it ought to be true, then it is true--such is the inferential logic used by the true believer. (See pp. 77-79)

FAITH. James suggests that a broad definition of a religious life consists of faith in an unseen order, and the consequent adjusting of oneself to this order. This "religious attitude", cannot be readily understood. He repeats Immanuel Kant's theory that such things are not objects of knowledge, and that they cannot be understand with the intellect. And yet, they can have deep meaning for the practice of religion. "We can act as if there were a God; lay plans as if we were immortal, and find a genuine difference in our moral life. Faith that these things actually exist allows us to act as if we knew what they might be, should we be allowed to conceive them. Thus we have a mind believing in the reality of a set of things of which the mind can form no real notion." Personal religion, for James, is an affair of faith, based either on vague sentiment (which is a dishonest religion), or upon a vivid sense of the reality of things unseen. Neither science nor philosophy can explain it—faith is only explainable by the fact of personal experience. (See pp. 58-60, 329, 346-347)

## *JAMES E. TALMAGE*

*A Study of the Articles of Faith* (1899, reprint ed. 42nd, Deseret Book, 1982)
The *Articles of Faith* is a compilation of Talmage's many lectures delivered at "the Church University and other schools." Talmage's stated purpose was to provide "an incentive and serviceable guide to earnest investigation of the Gospel of the Lord Jesus Christ" (Preface to 12th Edition).

Talmage takes as his subject the list of Articles of Faith of the Church, adopted in 1890 as "a guide in faith and conduct." The Articles of Faith present important doctrines, but do not necessarily represent a complete exposition of Mormon belief since the Church teaches the principle of continuing revelation.

THE NATURE OF FAITH. Talmage often quotes scripture to explain faith, e.g., Paul's "Now faith is the substance of things hoped for, the evidence of things not seen" (Heb. 11-1). Talmage then proceeds to define the correct meaning of the quoted scripture, e.g., Paul's word "substance" means "confidence or assurance", and "evidence" means "the demonstration of proof." Talmage addresses faith only as it pertains to the "full confidence and trust in the being, words, and objectives of God and Christ" (p. 96) And full confidence and trust remove all doubt concerning the things of God.

The personal faith Talmage describes may exist in persons in varying degrees—"Faith may manifest itself from the incipient state which is little more than feeble belief, scarcely free from hesitation and fear, to the strength of abiding confidence that sets doubt and sophistry at defiance" (p.97).

FAITH, BELIEF, AND KNOWLEDGE. Each term has a specific meaning to Talmage, although in scriptural usage little distinction is recognized and noted. Belief, however, is for Talmage "passive, an agreement or acceptance only; faith is active and positive, embracing such reliance and confidence as will lead to works"(p.97).

Faith in Christ is belief in Christ coupled with trust. As such one cannot have faith without some belief. Indeed, faith is vitalized living belief. Furthermore, faith is a prerequisite to salvation, a saving power.

Knowledge is described as superior belief, neither of which is sufficient to provide salvation. Having knowledge does not assure a better life of more understanding. Knowledge is to wisdom what belief is to faith—the former are abstract, the latter living applications.

HOW TO BUILD FAITH. Unlike many other writers, Talmage suggests ways to develop faith. The major requirement is "acceptance of God's will as our law, and of his words as our guide" (p. 100). Every being is blessed with some measure of faith—"One's faith may be weak and imperfect, for his ability to recognize the evidence upon which belief in God depends may be small. From trustworthy evidence, rightly interpreted, true faith will spring" (p. 100).

Faith, based upon evidence and rightful conclusions, is strengthened largely by the number of credible witnesses. "However improbable a declaration may appear to us, if the truth of it be affirmed by witnesses in whom we have confidence, we are led to admit the statement, at least provisionally, is true" (p. 101). For example, how does one who has never been to Washington know of the city, of the President, or of the authority of government? He will hear the testimony of those who have been there, see the pictures and books describing the place, and will learn of the laws emanating from the place. Inferences and evidence mount and develop into conviction. He acquires faith in the existence of a center of national government. This approach leads to the inevitable comparison to the question of the existence and authority of God. Holy men in ancient and modern times testify of him and teach his ways. Thus the foundation of faith in God is the belief and knowledge of him as "sustained" by holy testimony and authoritative declarations.

FAITH AS POWER. For Talmage faith is power. It is the very motive force by which people act. Students would not study if they had no faith in the possibility of success following study; farmers would not plant without the faith of a harvest. "Remove man's faith in the possibility of any desired success and you rob him of the incentive to strive. Faith is the secret of ambition, the soul of heroism, the motive power of effort" (p. 103).

FAITH IS CONDITIONAL. A conscious effort to live in accordance with the laws of God is essential to exercising a personal faith in God. If a man knows he is sinning, he will deprive himself of faith, and estranges himself from God. Furthermore, without faith, an essential to salvation, it is impossible to please God. "Christ's words on the matter are conclusive: 'He that believeth and is baptized shall be saved; but that believeth not shall be damned'" (p. 106). Talmage adds that faith is a gift of God, but "it is given only to those who show by their sincerity that they are worthy of it, and who give promise of abiding by its dictates" (p. 107). And without works, faith will die as expressed by James in the New Testament.

Talmage closes by denying the Protestant claim to salvation by grace. "Yet in spite of the plain word of God, dogmas of men have been promulgated to the effect that by faith alone may salvation be attained, and that a wordy profession of belief shall open the doors of heaven to the sinner. The scriptures cited and man's inherent sense of justice furnish a sufficient refutation of these false assertions" (p. 108).

Of interest is Talmage's quote (in the appendix) from a letter from J. M. Sjodahl, co-author of *The Doctrine and Covenants Commentary*, related to the use of the nouns *faith* and *belief*, and the verb *"to believe"* in the Bible. "The Greek word 'pistis' has been translated 'faith' 235 times and 'belief' once. We have no English verb for faith, but use 'to believe' which by derivation means 'to live.' In our language 'to believe' certainly admits of degrees of assurance, (from the slightest perception to the fullest assurance)...but that is not the way it is used in the Bible by the original authors. In their vocabulary 'belief' is full assurance and 'to believe' is 'to live' accordingly" (p. 479).

## *BERTRAND RUSSELL*

*The Will to Doubt* (New York, Philosophical Library, 1958)

In this 125-page collection of essays, Bertrand Russell pits his skeptical nature against all obstacles to a reasoned and rational way of life. His wrath is kindled against the orthodox, the powerful, the unthinking, the rich, those who rely on feelings over intellect, and anyone he feels stands in the way of reason.

ORIGINS OF BELIEF. Russell is the champion of rational thinking, which he defines as the "habit of taking account of all relevant evidence in arriving at a belief. Where certainty is unattainable, a rational man will give weight to the most probable opinion, while retaining others, which have an appreciable probablility, in his mind as hypotheses which subsequent evidence may show to be preferable" (pp. 9-10).

For those who have read the summary of Orson Pratt's "True Faith," this call for evidence will sound familiar. Yet I see these two men as opposites. What then of their similar demand for evidence to establish truth? In Pratt's case, acceptable evidence includes all sources: desire, tradition, testimony, feelings, intellectual conclusion, sensory input, revelation, inspiration, and the voice of authority, among others. Russell rejects all sources of evidence which are not rational, objective, scientific, or observable with the physical senses: "It is this kind of objective truth—a mundane and pedestrian affair—that is sought in science. It is this kind also that is sought in religion so long as people hope to find it. It is only when people have given up the hope of proving that religion is true in a straight forward sense that they set to work to prove that it is "true" in some (other) sense. It may be laid down broadly that irrationalism, i.e., disbelief in objective fact, arises almost always from the desire to assert something for which there is no evidence, or to deny something for which there is good evidence" (p. 11). Russell suggests that many religious beliefs are often contrary to fact and based on wishes, prejudice, fear, or traditions.

Russell does not hide his distain for religions and religious faith. "I am myself a dissenter from all known religions, and I hope that every kind of religious belief will die out. I do not believe that, on balance, religious belief has been a force for good" (p. 18). He believes that religions belong to the infancy of human reason and that they will eventually die out. He states that religions not only promulgate erroneous beliefs, but that they stifle free thinking and the free exchange of ideas. He champions the right for "free competition" between differing beliefs; he defends the right for one to state his beliefs with no penalty for differing from others.

DOUBT. William James coined the phrase, "will to believe." Russell supports and urges the "will to doubt." He observes that those not in power, not rich, and not in the group "dare not be frank in their beliefs" (p. 21). As for certainty, no one's beliefs are quite true; no one can know of a surety that they are. All have at least a shade of vagueness or the slight possibility of error. "The methods of increasing the degree of truth in our beliefs are well known; they consist of hearing all sides, trying to ascertain all the relevant facts, controlling our own bias by discussion with people who have the opposite bias, and cultivating a readiness to discard any hypothesis which has proved inadequate" (p. 22). He notes that in the scientific method, where something approximating genuine knowledge can be found, scientists' attitudes remain tentative and questioning.

Russell asks, "If it can be admitted that a condition of rational doubt would be desirable, why is there so much irrational certainty in the world?" (p. 23). He assigns the blame to human nature, credulity, state- or church-supported education, propaganda, and economic pressure. Education is indicted because it teaches facts, not ideas; ways of doing, not ways of thinking; and falsehoods, not truth (e.g., in faith-promoting and patriotism-promoting history, truth is not always the primary concern). Russell suggests that education should "have two objects: first to give definite knowledge, and second, to create mental habits which allow people to make sound judgments for themselves. [But today] it is not desired that people should think for themselves, because it is felt that people who think for themselves are awkward to manage and cause administrative difficulties. Only the *guardians*, in Plato's language, are to think; the rest are to obey, or to follow the leaders like sheep" (pp. 26-28).

Propaganda stifles rational thought because its appeal is usually to irrational causes of belief rather than to serious arguments of both sides of an issue. It also gives an advantage to those who can afford it—the rich and powerful. If rational thought is to have a chance, if there is to be any freedom of thought, then equality of opportunity among opinions is essential. Russell strongly (but naively) believes that people will choose the right, given all the facts in an unemotional atmosphere.

The other hinderance, economic pressure, is again a weapon waged by the powerful and rich against the poor and weak. It is necessary for the average person, if he or she wants to make a living, to avoid incurring the hostility of certain powerful individuals. Likewise, one can only remain a member of a group, social or economic, if he or she adheres to the group rules, rules which are laid down by the strongest of the group.

Russell takes pains to disengage himself from scientific findings only, I feel, and to associate himself with the scientific method. "My plea is for the spread of the scientific temper, which is different from the knowledge of scientific results. The scientific temper is capable of regenerating mankind" (p. 36).

He proposes only one "doctrine": *It is undesirable to believe a proposition when there is no evidence whatever for supposing it is true* (p. 38). This seems reasonable enough, but we must remember that Russell rejects all evidence except that which is objective, repeatable, sensible, and scientific. Strangely, he again makes a statement almost identical to James E. Talmage's suggestion that the testimony of reliable witnesses should take precedence, and almost in the same words--". . . the opinion of experts, when it is unanimous, must be accepted by non-experts as more likely right than the opposite opinion" (p. 39). And he suggests three rules to live by--

"(1) . . . when the experts are agreed, then the opposite opinion cannot be held to be certain; (2) when they are agreed, no opinion can be regarded as certain by a non-expert; and (3) when they all hold that no evidence for a positive opinion exists, the ordinary man would do well to suspend his judgement." (p. 39)

His distrust of non-objective, emotions-derived evidence is heavy. "The opinions that are held with passion are always those for which no good ground exists; indeed the passion is the measure of the holder's lack of rational conviction. Opinions in religion are almost always held passionately. (And) people hate skeptics far more than they hate the passionate advocates of opinions hostile to their own." (p. 40)

BELIEFS AS A SOURCE OF ACTION. Russell suggests that most of life is driven by habit and instinct, but that the most important decisions are based on belief--a man marries a woman believing she is something special; a woman invests in a stock believing that the company is sound and that the investment will pay off; a man supports a religious tenet believing it to be true. He further suggests that many of our beliefs are based on insufficient objective evidence--particularly as they relate to marriage, investments, religion, and other important personal activities.

FAITH AND BELIEF. Russell mixes his usage of faith and belief. He suggests that modern faith is not of "the same intensity of belief as was possible for St. Thomas Aquinas." This reduction of "faith intensity" is attributed to the greater intellectual influences on life, to the increase of objective evidence about the reality of nature, and to the present-day concern about the effects of religion in the world as opposed to concern about the after-life. "By subordinating God to the needs of this sublunary life, (people) cast suspicion upon the genuineness of their faith. They think that God, like the Sabbath, was made for man." (p.53) Belief and personal faith are seldom determined by rational motives, and the same is true of disbelief and nihilism, though religious skeptics often overlook this aspect.

Russell questions the validity of personal beliefs and suggests that people's conscious beliefs (or faith) are not consistent with their unconsious beliefs. He uses death as an example, stating that the belief that death is a gateway to a better life ought logically to prevent men from feeling the fear of death. But to the contrary, believers in an after-life are no less afraid of death or more courageous than those who hold no such belief or faith. The discrepancy seems to be that religious beliefs are held in the conscious mind, and they have not been able to alter the true beliefs of the unconcious mind.

TRUTH AND KNOWLEDGE. Russell relates that truth was absolute in his youth. He accepted that view and went about searching for "the truth" with gusto. Unfortunately, he says, his search was ruined by psychology, pragmatism, behavioral sciences, and Einsteins's relativity physics. In the old days the body was known to be matter, the spirt (or mind) immaterial and eternal. Everybody knew that—it was obvious to any rational man. Now along comes science which says that matter is really empty space, made up of unknown particles floating in a void, particles which will probably turn out to be simply energy. And the seemingly eternal mind turns out to be bio-chemical in nature, subject to the laws of chemistry. Can memory survive death when all the memory retaining chemistry disappears at death?

As for knowledge, it is "coming to be regarded not as a good in itself, or as a means of creating a broad and humane outlook on life in general, but as merely an ingredient in technical skill" (p. 72). "Useless" knowledge, which is driven by curiosity and knowledge that is not directly related to job or skill, when successfully integrated into the personality, forms a person's character, thought processes, and desires, and makes it possible for him to be of use socially. "Perhaps the most important advantage of "useless" knowledge is that it promotes a contemplative habit of mind (p. 77). "Curious learning not only makes unpleasant things less unpleasant, but also makes pleasant things more pleasant" (p. 78). Curious learning and useless knowledge are also the keys to enhancing productive doubting.

## PAUL TILLICH

*Dynamics of Faith* (New York: Harper and Row, 1957)

*Dynamics of Faith* represents one of the major works on the defense of faith written this century. Tillich's stated purpose is to reinterpret the confusing and multitudinous meanings attached by centuries of tradition to the simple act of personal faith: "There is hardly a word in the language which is subject to more misunderstandings, distortions, and questionable definitions than the word 'faith'. Today the word is more productive of disease than of health. It confuses, misleads, creates alternately skepticism and fanaticism, intellectual resistance and emotional surrender, rejection of religion and subjection to substitutes" (Introductory remarks).

PERSONAL FAITH. Tillich suggests that personal faith should be considered as one's Ultimate Concern. If all other concerns are subject to this ultimate concern, then this type of faith promises total fulfillment. A good example of this is the ultimate concern of many LDS—God the Father. He (God) is the One in whose name the great commandment is given: "Love the Lord thy God with all your heart, mind, and strength." These words describe the character of Tillich's faith—the demand of total surrender to the subject of ultimate concern. There can be no faith without a *content* to which it is directed—faith must always have a purpose. Unfortunately, some put their ultimate concern in money, power, status, other people, sex, and so forth.

This approach may, on first reading, seem narrow, cold, methodical, and inflexible. But Tillich proceeds throughout the rest of the book to soften, humanize, enliven, enrich, and personalize his definition of faith. For Tillich, faith as ultimate concern is the commitment of the total person, the emotional, the intellectual, and the physical. The ultimate concern becomes the center of life and includes all life's elements. Faith thus becomes the most personal and intimate of all personal acts, unconscious and conscious, and freely performed. However, "faith is not a creature of the will. In the ecstasy of faith the will to accept and to surrender is an element, but not the cause. And this is true also of feeling. Faith is not an emotional ouburst; certainly faith is in it, as in every act of spiritual life, but emotion does not produce faith" (pp.1-10). The ultimate concern gives depth, direction, and unity to all other concerns, and to the entire personality of the person.

FAITH AND DOUBT. The act of faith is the finite turning to the infinite. Faith may be certain at the finite level, but must be uncertain at the infinite level. The element of uncertainty in faith is unremovable, and must be accepted as part of any act of faith. It takes courage to accept uncertainty. But where there is courage there is the potential for failure. In every act of faith this risk of failure must be taken (with possibly devastating results if the faith act fails.) The courage of faith is made possible because people "are never able to bridge the infinite distance between the infinite and the finite from the side of the finite" (p. 105). But we are willing to take the risk of a faith act because even failure cannot separate us from our ultimate concern.

All this suggests the relation of faith to doubt: "If faith is understood as belief that something is true, doubt is incompatible with the act of faith. If faith is understood as being ultimately concerned, doubt is a necessary element in it. It is a consequence of the risk of faith. [But] the doubt which is implicit in faith is not a doubt about facts or conclusions. It is not the same as doubt which is the life blood of scientific research" (pp. 18-19). The doubt Tillich defines is neither one of skepticism, nor one of rejection. Rather, it is the doubt associated with risk. "It is not the permanent doubt of the scientist, and not the transitory doubt of the skeptic, but it is the doubt of him who is ultimately concerned...the existential doubt. [Faithful doubt] does not question whether a propostition is true or false. It does not reject truth, but is aware of the element of insecurity in truth. At the same time, the doubt of faith accepts this insecurity and takes it into itself in an act of courage" (p. 20).

Tillich's insight on doubt has a practical significance for Mormons who doubt. Many feel unwarranted guilt, anxiety, and despair about what they perceive as "a loss of faith." Better understood, doubt is a confirmation of faith, suggesting the unconditional nature of the ultimate concern.

Some have suggested that there is a quiet certainty associated with faith that results in a lack of doubt. And one finds in the faithful a serenity of life. But among those for whom such a state as been achieved—saints and others firm in their faith—an element of undeniable doubt still remains.

Tillich asks an important question for members of the Church: "Can a community of faith, e.g., a church, accept a faith which includes doubt as an intrinsic element and calls the seriousness of doubt an expression of faith? And even if it could allow such an attitude in its ordinary members, could it permit the same in its leaders?" (p. 23). Such an attitude would be foreign to Mormonism in the 1980s, I suspect.

FAITH AND KNOWLEDGE. Tillich suggests that faith is regularly misinterpreted as "knowledge that has a low degree of evidence." In this meaning, faith is mistaken for belief. "Knowledge is a matter of inquiry by ourselves or those we trust. Almost all the struggles between faith and knowledge are rooted in the wrong understanding of faith as a type of knowledge which has a low degree of evidence but is supported by religious authority" (p. 33).

FAITH AND BELIEF. Belief is related more to knowledge than to faith. Tillich writes, "No command to believe and no will to believe can create faith. This is important for religious education. One should never convey the impression that faith is a demand made upon them, the rejection of which is lack of good will. Finite man cannot produce infinite concern. Our will cannot produce the certainty which belongs to faith. Neither arguments for belief nor the will to believe can create faith" (p.36-38) Unfortunately, Tillich offers no sure method for creating faith.

FAITH AND REASON. For Tillich, reason and faith (as ultimate concern) do not conflict because reason supplies the tools for controlling reality, and faith supplies the direction in which control may be exercised: ". . . reason is identical with the humanity of man. It is the basis of language, freedom, and creativity. It is involved in the search for knowledge, the experience of art, and it makes a centered personal life possible. If faith were the opposite of reason, it would tend to dehumanize man. A faith which destroys reason destroys itself and the humanity of man, for a being of reason is able to be ultimately concerned . . . ."(pp. 74-77). As such, reason is the precursor to faith, and faith is the extension of reason beyond its achievable bounds.

FAITH AND ACTION. The actions of faith—its "dynamics"—are found in the tensions between participation and separation of the faithful person and his or her ultimate concern. But without participation, one cannot be concerned about it. Likewise, the faithful person must be separated from the objects of his or her faith. Otherwise, it would be a matter of certainty, not of faith. Participation encourages the coming of certainty; separation engenders doubt.

Faith also affects life's action by uniting the mental life and by giving it a dominating center. It becomes the discipline which regulates daily life; it encourages contemplation and thinking; it enables one to concentrate on ordinary work or on other human beings; it supports love and its activities.

Faith is concerned with the desires and activities of love; it is the object of unconditional love, it fuels the love of God and man. Faith is "love in a sense of the desire for reunion with that to which one belongs. Love and action are ... not external to faith [as it would be if faith were less than ultimate concern] but are elements of the concern itself. The separation of faith and love is always the consequence of the deterioration of religion" (pp. 99-115).

For Tillich, love is action just as faith is action; faith implies love; and the expression of love is action. The real link between faith and works is love.

## *ERIC HOFFER*

*The True Believer* (New York: Harper and Row, 1951)

Hoffer's first successful book, *The True Believer*, is about fanatics in mass movements. I include a comment or two here for the purpose of distinguishing the religious believer—the type we are interested in—from the fanatical adherent to a mass movement who is prepared to die for the cause. These latter True Believers are prepared to accept unquestioning blind faith as the entrance fee to the group.

There is, of course, a certain similarity between types of faith, types of dedication to a cause, types of self-sacrifice, and types of acceptance. But there are differences too, and these predominate. Hoffer's true believer has fanatical faith, is ready to sacrifice life for a holy cause, and is frustrated to extremes with life as it is. The religious believer is one tuned in to himself and his realtionship to God and humanity. Religious belief coupled with faith brings independence, an independence which frees the person to do good and love others. Hoffer's true believer loses his independence in the corporateness of the mass movement and finds only the freedom to hate, bully, torture, murder, and lie—all without guilt or remorse.

We might find occasional Hoffer-brand true believer involved in the Church, but they would find themselves unwelcome and aliènated from the main stream.

## *RICHARD C. POLL*

"What the Church Means to Me," *Dialogue: A Journal of Mormon Thought* (vol. 2, Winter 1968): pp. 107-117; "Liahona and Iron Rod Revisited," *Dialogue* (vol. 18, Spring 1985): pp 69-78

Richard Poll, a retired BYU professor of history, originally presented the 1968 essay at a Palo Alto ward sacrament meeting. This seminal paper has also appeared in the RLDS *Saints' Herald* and *Sunstone*, and over 2,500 re-prints have been distributed. Poll's metaphors for Mormon faithful—Iron Rods and Liahonas—have become well-worn terms among Latter-day Saints. His 1985 essay offers additional insights.

In the earlier essay, Poll suggested that there are two different types of active Mormons, both of whom are dedicated and faithful to the gospel. Unfortunately, each is skeptical and suspicious of the other's dedication and commitment to the Church. Poll states that his purpose in writing is to help move both kinds of Mormons toward a "unity of faith." In the later essay, he says his purpose in writing is to promote tolerance and mutual understanding.

The metaphor for one type is the Iron Rod from Lehi's dream; the second derives from the same dream—the Liahona. The Iron Rod is the sure word of God, while the Liahona was a guiding compass. Both describe ways of approaching the gospel.

For the Iron Rod person, each step along the journey of life is facilitated by keeping his or her hand on the rod; he or she has only to hold on. The way is not easy, but it is clear. For the Liahona, life's direction is not so clear. The Liahona points in the right direction, but the clarity of the path varies with the person's vision and understanding. These questions illuminate the difference: Do the revelations of God provide a handrail or a compass? Is the gospel prescriptive or suggestive?

Poll says that Iron Rod members do not look for questions but for answers. And the gospel has all the answers. Liahona members, on the other hand, are preoccupied with questions and are skeptical of pat answers. They don't see all the answers but accept those they find. They find enough to motivate and give direction to their lives. The problem arises because Iron Rod members see a questioning attitude as an imperfect faith and commitment; Liahona members see an unquestioning spirit as naive and dangerous, particularly if an erroneous belief is accepted as fact.

Poll offers no convincing explanation as to why or how these two types evolve. He suggests that conversion processes, education, upbringing, parents, the preexistence, and life's experiences may all influence the outcome. And no one selects the type he or she will be; it just happens. However, Poll observes that people may move from one extreme to the other, more commonly from Iron Rod to Liahona. He also acknowledges that a continuum exists—people don't fit simply into only one of the two extremes. He also suggests that a person may be an Iron Rod in some respects and a Liahona in others.

Confronted with matters of faith and belief, Iron Rod members pray for answers and frequently get them. Liahona members pray for strength to cope with uncertainty, and for understanding, and they frequently have those prayers answered. Iron Rod members pray for knowledge; Liahonas pray for faith.

The Iron Rod member is convinced that the "mind and will of the Lord may be obtained" on any subject through scripture, authority, and the Holy Spirit (p. 110, 1968). The Liahona, lacking this confidence, is skeptical of the three sources: Scriptures are not always inspired and may contain mistakes. Authorities differ and make mistakes. Blindly following anything as subjective as "the burning in the bosom" is fraught with danger.

Iron Rod members consequently may develop answers where none exist. This confidence in personal insights may make them dogmatic, impatient, and inflexible—even in the face of new revelation. Liahonas, on the other hand, are often led to broaden their questioning and doubting until "even the most clearly defined Church doctrines and policies are included" (p. 112, 1968). They may be drawn into carping criticism of Church leaders, and their ties to the Church may become nebulous and meaningless. They may become hypocritical in their own eyes, and their testimonies may become so selective that they serve only as an emotional defense.

It is Poll's hopeful observations that both types serve the Church, that both hold positions of responsibility, and both find programs and policies they can identify with. It is not a queston of black hats vs. white hats. Virtue and vice can be found in individuals in both groups. In matters of doctrinal opinion, "the distinction is discernible in responses to the question: Is the more reliable test of the validity of a statement its substance or its source?" (p. 72, 1985). Iron Rod members see authorities and scripture as the more important; Liahonas see the substance of the proposition as more important—Is it reasonable? Is it true? Is it useful? Will it work? Is there something better?

In his 1985 essay, Poll suggests that whether a person identifies with either group is not particularly critical. Indeed, the need may never arise, because "a typical LDS commitment is not to a set of rigorously examined truth propositions, but to a collection of activities, values, attitudes, hopes, customs, emotions, support systems, and verbal and visual symbols" (p. 73, 1985). Sharing many of these components of testimony, Latter-day Saints who see themselves as Iron Rod members or Liahona members "can abide each other without difficulty as long as they have the spirit of Christ" (p. 78, 1985)

## *FRANCISCO JOSE MORENO*

*Between Faith and Reason: Basic Fear and the Human Condition* (New York: Harper/Colophon Books, 1977)

The subtitle of this 130-page book is drawn from Moreno's observation that much of human activity and thought is generated by what he calls basic fear. With basic fear, it is difficult to identify the threat; not knowing causes the fear. For example, fear of darkness is not the same as fear in an impending auto crash where we know the source and the outcome of the tragedy; we perceive the threat and it is a real threat. Feelings of anxiety, apprehension, and insecurity are caused by basic fear. Reasoning and thinking about the unknown arouse basic fear because reason asks questions which may have no rational, observable answers. Thus "basic fear results from our humanness" because humans alone can reason (p. 7).

A common reaction to basic fear is to repress or avoid the unknown, or to deny the associated feelings. We may move the painful and troublesome emotions from the conscious mind to the unconscious. We may try to find comfort in answers that are not based on reason, i.e., we find answers in faith and in the voices of authority found in religion. We are willing to accept "non-rational" answers. (Moreno uses non-rational in the place of irrational because he wants to dissassociate his meaning from the connotations of incoherence and absurdity which irrational has acquired. Non-rational means that the answer is not founded on modern rules of reason and scientific inquiry.)

BELIEFS. All religions have formed around a list of beliefs (a creed) and a group of ceremonies. Moreno defines creed as a list of answers to the unknowable questions: What is the purpose of life? Where did we come from and where will we go after death? Why must we die? General principles ("God exists") Moreno calls *values*; specific points of doctrine ("God has a body") he calls *beliefs*. The distinction is not always clear, but the basic difference is that values do not change, while beliefs may vary without overturning values. ("God could exist outside his body.") Creeds vary with the times and seasons.

And so we see religions being formed to answer rational questions which cannot satisfactorily be explained through reason and objective evidence. "The question as to who made the universe is the result of a rational process. In our experience we see things being created and we observe a certain logical sequence from their beginning to their end. We apply rational logic to our experience and observations and ask who or what created us. A religious answer to the question can be accepted only by the suspension of rational logic. 'God created the universe' is a non-rational answer because the acceptance of this answer depends on faith and trust rather than on any logically demonstrated proof. A nonrational answer to a rational question is thus produced in order to satisfy our emotional need for security. The religious answer is accepted through an inner intuitive perception which does not depend on the rational process. In other words, the validity of the answer does not rely on whether or not we can find out if the universe was actually created by God, but on whether we believe it to be so. As those in religion never tire of saying, the truth is not acquired through reason, but through faith" (p. 85).

**FAITH.** Faith, for Moreno, is the suspension of our rational abilities and the acceptance of non-rational answers to our unanswerable questions. One can exercise faith in areas other than religion. Falling in love is an act of faith, for example. Moreno acknowledges the confusing multiplicity of meanings for *faith,* but states that his work is restricted to personal faith, "a phenomenon that takes place in the individual mind. Even when faith is expressed collectively, its essence remains individual" (p. 86). Moreno describes faith as the bridge between a rational question and a non-rational answer.

Although we may be willing to suspend the rational as an integral part of an act of faith, this does not mean that we completely lose our ability to reason. In fact, once we have established faith, we use reason to defend and explain it. "We use reason to defend what we believe in, but not to question the validity of the act of faith itself" (p. 88). Unfortunately, reasoning and thinking about the unanswerable questions raise basic fear. Therefore, we use faith to defend against basic fear. Each person develops a strategy for coping with the insecurity. "The development of this strategy is not a conscious act on our part, and it is affected by the historical, social, and cultural circumstances of our birth, as well as by our own individual circumstances. This strategy consists of placing our faith in certain ideas, objects, or people so that we can rely on them--unthinkingly--to give a purpose, meaning, and justification to our lives" (p. 89). This strategy is not dependent upon a single article of faith, or limited to a single part of life. We organize our objects of faith. We are also careful to leave an escape route. If one source of security comes under attack, we replace it with others. "Someone whose dependence upon religion is undermined, for example, might react by trying to increase the security he gets from children, job, politics, or something else" (p. 91). The alternative to finding a substitute is an undesirable increase of basic fear and its pain. Thus, according to Moreno, we are likely to adhere to the ways of faith, even though we may alter the articles of faith.

FAITH AND REASON. Reason and faith are somewhat incompatible, although reason may used to justify already-determined beliefs. But reason introduces a dilemma: the more reason we use and the more rational we are, the more difficult it becomes to apply faith. This increases basic fear, which in turn urges us back to faith and away from reason. People move back and forth, making forays into the unknown of reason for a season, only to scurry back to the comfort of faith. The crisis generated by reason is softened, giving us strength to explore the frontier again. This cycle has powerful reinforcements at each end, and each healthy person achieves a balance, in accordance with his or her experience, education, and so forth.

It is Moreno's feeling that as much as we would like to, we cannot give up reasoning altogether. If we could, life might be easier, but much duller.

## *JAMES W. FOWLER*

*STAGES OF FAITH -- The Psychology of Human Development and the Quest for Meaning* (New York: Harper and Row, 1981)

James W. Fowler has written a monumental and enlightening book on the subject of faith--must reading for all who are curious about religion.

This is the golden age of classification. Mormons are classified, for example, as active and inactive, full or part tithe payers, recommend holders, closet doubters, and so forth. James Fowler has attempted the ultimate--classifying the mystifying miracle of personal faith as practiced by the world's diverse faithful.

Building upon the ideas of pioneers James, Tillich, Niebuhr, and Kohlberg, and based on his own studies since 1972, Fowler suggests it is possible to assign the faithful to one of six groups, or faith stages, through which people move as they mature.

Through hundreds of interviews, Fowler has tentatively validated the first four stages. However, he found that faith is a continuum, stretching like a series of slopes and plateaus from sea level to misty heights of the tallest mountains, with six grand steppes where people tend to congregate. Fowler has found few real people inhabiting the final two stages, the last of which he assigns such persons as Gandhi and Mother Teresa. However, Fowler's first four stages are crowded.

Mormons of all shades will recognize themselves and others on one of the plateaus, or struggling up the rocky trail between stages. Those interested in Iron Rods, Liahonas, Closet Doubters, conversion mechanics, and other mysteries of personal faith will be interested in this book.

Fowler devotes the first 116 pages of the book to narrowing and precisely defining faith in a personal sense (as opposed to such uses as faith as a religion, faith as a system of beliefs, faith as honesty, and so forth). Fowler identifies personal faith with trust, hope, and fidelity. According to Fowler, Western culture has managed over the centuries to obscure the simplicity of personal faith, resulting in much misunderstanding, heartache, and personal guilt.

THE SIX STAGES The final 207 pages of the book are devoted to describing Fowler's six stages of faith. Stage One faith is a fantasy-filled, initiating phase, usually experienced only in childhood, where a person is permanently influenced by the examples, moods, stories, and symbols of visible belief systems. Here are formed the taboos, the participatory habits, the cultural expectations, and the symbolisms of the religion. Fowler's description of an adult in Stage One faith will be recognized by many Mormons (but with uneasiness): "For every child whose significant others shared religion in ways that proved life-opening and sustaining of love, faith, and courage, there is another for whom the introduction of religion gave rise to fear, rigidity, and the brutalization of souls. This often results in the emergence of an adult with a very rigid, brittle and authoritarian personality" (p. 132, condensed).

In Stage Two, a person moves away from fantasizing, but appropriates stories, beliefs, morals, and symbols in a one-dimensional, literal way. Persons in Stage Two see the world as based only on reciprocal fairness and justice: blessings are predicated on obedience, misfortunes derive from sin, life is a formula. Fowler's discussion of an adult Stage Two person will be familiar: "The limitations of literalness and excessive reliance upon reciprocity as a principle for constructing an ultimate environment can result either in an overcontrolling, stilted perfectionism, or in their opposite, an abasing sense of badness embraced because of mistreatment, neglect or the apparent disfavor of significant others" (p. 150, condensed).

Stage Three is characteristic of many Mormons. It's structure is influenced strongly by interpersonal relationships. It is conformist in that the person is acutely tuned into the expectations and judgements of others. The Stage Three person has adopted a cluster of beliefs and values, but rarely reflects on or examines them systematically.

Authority rests in worthy others. Faith has provided a comfortable basis for outlook and personal identity.

Stage Four faith is characterized by the tensions of: (1) group definition vs. individuality; (2) subjectivity and unexamined feelings vs. objectivity and critical self-reflection; (3) living for others vs. self-fulfillment; and (4) the importance of absolutes vs. relatives. For Stage Four persons, religious symbols lose their literalness and are translated into conceptual meanings. The self, no longer sustained mostly by others, adopts an independence in reactions, interpretations, and judgements of external and internal events. Authority and responsibility pass from others to self. Stage Four people feel conflict, see irony in life, and experience the pulls and tensions of different points of view.

Stages Five and Six are reserved for the few, the mature, the saintly. Fowler uses such idealistic Stage Five descriptors as, "alive to the paradox and truth of contradictions ... unifies opposites in mind and experience ... commitment to justice is freed from the confines of class, nation, religion, and community" (pp. 197-198 ) Stage Six is said to be characterized by "perfect love, lack of division, universalizing faith, being heedless of threats to self," and other idealizations.

Fowler has reasonably managed to describe stages or classes of faith and has demonstrated the existence of persons at least compatible with the first four stages. Unfortunately, he has largely failed in his second task, that of explaining the personal development of faith. Three burning questions remain to be answered: (1) Why does one person sojourn in Stage Two or Three while another moves on to Stage Four without any apparent effort or intention to do so? (2) How do we motivate ourselves and others to progress from one stage to another? (3) Should we?

### *R. JAN STOUT*

"The Spectrum of Religious Beliefs and Behaviors in the Mormon Community," Essay presented at the Sunstone Theological Symposium, 1983)

R. Jan Stout, a Mormon psychiatrist, begins his essay by stating that the formation of beliefs and religious practices is highly complex, and is beyond the scope of his essay. Recognizing that, he restricts his examination of Mormon beliefs to the influence of anxiety on the development of personal religious orientation.

THE PROBLEM OF ANXIETY. According to Stout, anxiety can be

divided into three basic forms: separation anxiety, castration anxiety, and existential anxiety. Studies have suggested that each form plays a significant role in the development of our minds. Each form is intertwined with basic religious questions: How do we explain and cope with life and death? and so forth.

Separation anxiety is the most fundamental of the tension-producing mental states. An infant encounters this anxiety when mother does not respond when he or she cries or calls. The child feels alone, vulnerable, and abandoned. This separation must be endured repeatedly, and eventually numbed through denial and repression. We must struggle to acquire defenses.

Castration anxiety does not mean specific dismemberment. Rather, it is an anxiety that accompanies the fear of punishment and retribution. We become aware of our lack of power and our need to seek support. We may have transgressed against an authority figure and desperately want to escape the wrath of his or her judgement. One solution may be to join a group for collective protection.

Existential anxiety arises when we confront the terror and uncertainty of a universe that seems awesome and unknowable. We see beyond the safety of our family a world full of risks, dangers, and unknowns. When we experience existential anxiety, we have looked beyond the predicable to a new and challenging frontier.

THE DEVELOPMENT OF RELIGIOUS TYPES. Stout suggests that we can identify four groups of Mormons who seem to have arrived at their religious positions from the complex interplay of anxiety, social forces, and life experiences. The four types are (simplified):

- submissive and dependant (S&D)
- social and organizational (S&O)
- skeptic and individualistic (S&I)
- selfless and universal (S&U)

Each group determines, to a great extent, the way its members view God and the universe, and contributes to expectations of rewards, judgement, and exhaltation.

We may assign a person to a single group, but some traits of each group can be found in every person. The remainder of Stout's essay examines these four groups and the role anxiety plays in their development.

Submissive and Dependent (S&D) traits arise in response to separation anxiety. These people retain the basic orientation they learned as children. They have a strong need to please, submit, and obey to avoid the dreaded fear of abandonment. S&Ds are adept at scanning the horizon for cues that keep them safely in the center. Belief can become subservient to personal comfort. They live with their childhood habits, never asking significant questions; or they argue that God exists and religious activity is important, feeling that they have everything to gain and nothing to lose by believing. Among S&Ds there is a strong desire for unconditional love, and great emphasis is placed on "people-pleasing."

Stout suggests we should not take the separation anxiety too lightly or view it simply as infantile. Such anxiety is not reserved for S&D people only. Such feelings for God may be essential and appropriate. Certainly, overcoming separation is the central message of the Atonement. However, to remain only child-like and dependent is to deny the personal responsibility we all share to mature spiritually.

Social and Organizational (S&O) people value the group and their membership above all else. These Mormons find security and structure for their lives in Church organizations. They move towards authority figures and often like positions of power themselves. They fear losing control and dealing with powerful emotions. They are what Maslow calls "non-peakers" and "religious bureaucrats." Love may be considered conditional God is perceived as a loving father who rewards his children only when they have been dutiful, obedient, and faithful to the end.

For S&Os, the core anxiety revolves around punishment, loss of power, and impotence—the "castration" anxiety. Obedience to a strong authority can help relieve this anxiety. Religious rituals and order become important, and attention to detail (proficiency in scriptural recall, for example) is highly coveted. These people play an important role in the organizational structure of the Church and through their hard work, loyalty, and obedience, often rise to levels of considerable authority.

Skeptic and Individualistic (S&I) people have had to learn to deal with existential anxiety. Formulas that seemed to work in childhood for answering the religious questions of life begin to falter. As one surveys the complexities of life and numerous uncertainties, doubts arise. Does God really intervene and answer prayers? What about God's other children who live in abject poverty or suffer miserable life situations? These types of questions gnaw at his or her conscience and generate even further questions and doubts.

For the S&I person there is a growing sense of individual responsibility rather than a reliance on the Church to answer all questions. For some this may be a time of rebellion against authority or against one's own submissive past.

Sketicism may appear in early life; it may be brief, or it may last a lifetime. Some Mormons successfully separate their religious life from their worldly life. They may develop powerful intellectual insights and technical knowledge, yet stay safely in one of the former two groups for their religion. For a few people, sudden personal tragedies or events (the unexplained death of a loved one, or reading and believing an anti-Mormon publication, for example) may catapult the person into the S&I group. The outcome is bewilderment, disillusionment, and feelings of betrayal. This may lead to "falling away," cynicism, or anti-Mormon behavior. Some may quietly abandon cherished spiritual rituals; others may evolve into closet doubters.

For S&I people, there can be an exhilarating sense of freedom in learning to live with doubt, uncertainty, and questions. There can be growth, courage, and the daring to explore new horizons. And yet, the danger of slipping into cynicism and the rejection of God is always there. For this reason, they may envy the certainty and security enjoyed by unquestioning Mormons. They may look back with nostalgia to a time when life was more predictable and secure.

The Selfless and Universal (S&U) person is not found in large numbers. While many may have had brief membership in this group, it is an elusive stage and difficult to maintain. The first three groups are characterized by individual self-awareness and self-consciousness, concern with personal salvation, preservation of power, and awareness of their own intellectual life. S&U people have been able to move beyond these concerns. They become aware of feelings of wholeness and comprehend the unity of all things. Their concern for their fellows overcomes their own narrow self-interests. They understand how to integrate all moral values into their lives, which become full of love and virtue. Anxieties are quieted and the person comes to terms with life, even though not all the answers are in.

Many Mormons can identify Church leaders and General authorities who personify the S&U person. These leaders inspire and touch lives in deep and significant ways. They recognize the traits of all groups within themselves, and can therefore love and accept the broad spectrum of Mormons.

CONCLUSION. Stout concludes that there is, and should be, ample room in the Mormon Church for all of stages, groups, and types of people desiring fellowship. Such diversity makes for a vigorous community. In accepting such conclusions, we can learn unity with all our fellow travelers on this planet, and we can experience the Selfless and Universalizing phenomenon more often.

### *RELATED THOUGHTS*

*You call for faith: I show you doubt, To prove that faith exists. The more of doubt, the stronger faith, I say, If faith o'ercomes doubt.*
—Robert Browning

*We are born believing. A man bears beliefs, as a tree bears apples.*
—Ralph Waldo Emerson

*All men naturally desire knowledge.*
—Aristotle

*The majority of mankind is lazy-minded, incurious...and tepid in emotion, and is therefore incapable of either much doubt or much faith.*
—T.S. Eliot

*Hope is the parent of faith.*
—Cyprus A. Bartol

*An appeal to reason has never been known to fail in the long run.*
—James Russel Lowell

*Skepticism is the chastity of the intellect.*
—George Santayana

*If the work of God could be comprehended by reason, it would be no longer wonderful, and faith would have not merit if reason provided proof.*
—St. Gregory

*Reason is one thing and faith is another, and reason can as little be made a substitute for faith, as faith can be made a substitute for reason.*
—Unknown

*The essence of belief is the establishment of a habit.*
—Charles S. Peirce

*It is always easier to believe than to deny. Our minds are naturally affirmative.*
—M. de Montalgne

*Most of our so-called reasoning consists of finding arguments for going on believing as we already do.*
—James Robinson

*In all things it is better to hope than to despair.*
—Johann Wolfgang von Goethe

*Truth above all, even when it upsets and overwhelms us.*
—Henri Amiel

*You believe easily that which you hope for earnestly.*
—Terence

*One person with a belief is equal to a force of 99 who have only interests.*
—John Stuart Mill

*Skepticism, riddling the faith of yesterday, prepares the way for the faith of tomorrow.*
—Romain Rolland

*Hope is the struggle of the soul breaking loose from what is perishable, and attesting her eternity.*
—Herman Melville